Dave Sommerich,
ordered from publisher
October 17, 1983;
received New York, January 20, 1984

RECOLLECTIONS OF A PIONEERING SOVIETOLOGIST

HAZARD ADDRESSING THE ROUNDTABLE IN MOSCOW, 1978

RECOLLECTIONS OF A PIONEERING SOVIETOLOGIST

By
JOHN N. HAZARD

OCEANA PUBLICATIONS, INC., NEW YORK • LONDON • ROME

Library of Congress Cataloging in Publication Data

Hazard, John N. (John Newbold), 1909-
   Recollections of a pioneering Sovietologist.

   Bibliography: p.
   Includes index.
   1. Hazard, John N. (John Newbold), 1909-
2. Lawyers—United States—Biography.
3. Sovietologists—United States—Biography.   I. Title
KF373.H392A37   1983   349.73'092'4 [B]   83-12132
ISBN 0-379-20047-3   347.300924 [B]

© Copyright 1984 by John N. Hazard

All rights reserved. No part of this publication may be reproduced or transmitted in any form or by any means, electronic or mechanical, including photocopy, recording, xerography, or any information storage and retrieval system, without permission in writing from the publisher.

Manufactured in the United States of America

TABLE OF CONTENTS

Foreword	vii
Prologue	ix
CHAPTER ONE Around the World	3
CHAPTER TWO Moscow Student Days	17
CHAPTER THREE Wall Street	31
CHAPTER FOUR Marriage and Family	41
CHAPTER FIVE The Lend-Lease Episode	49
CHAPTER SIX With the Vice-President	65
CHAPTER SEVEN Drafting the Nuremberg Indictment	81
CHAPTER EIGHT The Russian Institute Years	89
CHAPTER NINE The Church and its People	105
CHAPTER TEN Emeritus and All That	117
Bibliography	129
Chronology	133
Index	137

FOREWORD

How does one become a Sovietologist, and what does a Sovietologist do? Back in 1909 the question would have been unthinkable. Although the first soviets had emerged during the severe riots of 1905, the Tsar was still on his throne. The Russian Revolution was still eight years away, and even Russia, herself, seemed remote from the thoughts of Americans. Only a handful were concerned with diplomacy or business investments in the Empire. Scholarship on Russia was limited principally to historical studies, and even those were slanted toward Russia's relations with the West. Few cared to teach what was going on within the Empire itself.

The revolutionary events of 1917 introduced a change, but it moved slowly, especially in America. There was no recognition of the Soviet Government until 1933, and those who concerned themselves with things "soviet" were looked upon with suspicion by their fellow countrymen. Is it any wonder that when an opportunity to become a Sovietologist was offered to me in 1934, it seemed a risky speculation? What would one have to do to prepare for such a career, and what would one be likely to do in it, once preparation had passed its first stage? There were no blueprints drafted by those who had gone before. One had to approach the field as a pioneer venturing into the unknown with no tried and true plan of action.

Of course, the plan developed, more or less through trial and error, was influenced by personal preferences as well as by those who had the foresight to offer the opportunity to enter upon such a career. Those personal preferences had been developed from childhood and youthful experiences and probably rested on family background as well. No two persons would have approached the problems in the same way. And, what one did with the training in Moscow at the outset of the preparatory stage inevitably depended upon interests nurtured from childhood. Chance had much to do with developments as it does in shaping any career, but choices had to be made along the road, and those choices, often unconsciously, were dictated by what had gone before. Certainly the Second World War was a major factor among the chance events that had influence upon career possibilities, and the aftermath, although less dramatic, opened the way to still more opportunities. But, the decision might have been made to remain in the practice of law rather than to enter upon the life of an academic. Childhood experiences may well have foreordained the choice.

Because a career is cumulative—beginning unconsciously, of course, with childhood—this brief autobiography starts in 1909, long before Sovietology became a career, and proceeds to the postretirement stage since there are still things to do in response to invitations. No one could have anticipated what has happened, and, in retrospect, more than seventy years seem to be all of a piece as if they had been planned from the start. Of course, they are seen from the inside, from the man who has lived them. What an outsider might discern is another matter. A lawyer-journalist, formerly a student at Columbia University, is beginning such an assessment. This set of recollections is part of his documentation. Perhaps he will tell a different story, but until a conclusion is reached, this chronicle may throw some light on how to become a Sovietologist and what one does in the role.

J.N.H.

January 1983

PROLOGUE

The record of any individual can be read effectively when maturity is reached, achievements are evident, opinions have been expressed publicly to attract approval or dissent, character has been formed and honors bestowed. The record of the early years, in contrast, is unknown even to the individual concerned because much of the future of a child occurs before there is memory. No one begins to remember before the age of four or five, and what is seemingly remembered is little more than a romanticization of what was dimly perceived.

For a person born in 1909, there can be little before the outbreak of World War I to be recalled; however, some of those earliest years, as they have been reconstructed from tales told by parents or aging photographs, may serve as a prologue to what was to happen later. With such a caveat the story will begin.

Although the first recollection dates from July 1914, there were the obviously important events of birth. On that January 5, 1909, babies were not born in hospitals. They were brought into the world at home by a family doctor and a nurse. So it happened that Ada Bosarte DeKalb Hazard and John Gibson Hazard were delivered of their son, John Newbold Hazard, II. Their home was a massive red brick mansion with white porches standing among the stately elms of James Street in Syracuse, New York. The baby's father had moved from Rhode Island after graduating from Yale as a chemical engineer. It was at his job with the Solvay Process Company that John Gibson had met Ada. She was a southerner from an old Shenandoah family that moved north after the Civil War to escape the penury which would have been inevitable had they attempted to farm their plantation without tools or slaves. Indeed, as the boy was later to learn from his maternal grandmother, that move had been forced upon them by the fact that both the Gray and the Blue Armies had raced across the plantation night after night, threatening the family and stealing their food. Only that which was hidden under the bed in the laundry bag was saved to feed their son.

Fortunately, Ada's parents, Enoch DeKalb and his wife Emma, were people of fortitude and education. Enoch, like many another planter of the time, benefited from a classical education. Now he decided to move North, to Yankeeland, where money was said to be found among those who wanted to educate their children in the classics. After Emma and he began their journey, Ada Bosarte was born in Frederick, Maryland, the home of the legendary Barbara Fritchie, a woman who had defied the Gray troops during the war. It was Ada, born in adversity to a family that would not be downed, who took up the task in 1909 of rearing her child to meet the perils of what was to come. It was due to that experience that little John Newbold was introduced to the violin at an early age. Come what might, he would have a solid training in music. The belief was that the moving picture theaters would have to have music to accompany their silent films and music would provide an income for the boy just as the classics had saved the day for the DeKalb family when it fled the poverty of the postwar South and settled in the rich North.

Quite a different background was provided from the Hazard side. John Gibson was the second son of a wealthy mill-owner, John Newbold Hazard, I of Peace Dale, Rhode Island, the descendant of one of the founders of Newport, Rhode Island. That founder had broken with the Massachusetts Bay Colony because of the austerity it demanded of its settlers. He joined Anne Hutchinson, noted religious leader, and moved down Narragansett Bay to found a colony that would be more tolerant, although just as religious. From this colonial beginning, the family had become a pillar of Rhode Island and joined in every activity. They participated as both loyalists and revolutionaries during the Revolutionary War and shared in the continuing battle with the South over slavery. Indeed, one of the grandfathers of John Gibson had purchased slaves on his business trips to the South, before the Civil War, in order to free them. So the little boy of 1909 had within his own immediate family both liberators and slave owners. This fact was not left unnoticed as he grew up. Indeed, he was given, as a memento of the Civil War, two bayonets beaten by blacksmiths into hoes. The bayonets were picked up on the Shenandoah plantation so that a living might be eked out until the DeKalbs moved North.

1914 was the first memory, as has been said, and it was a curious one. It occurred on the stoop of a wooden house on a farm in Marcellus, New York. The children were taken there during the hot summer days to escape the city life of the family home in Syracuse. The little boy remembered being awakened by his grandmother, Emma DeKalb, in what seemed like the dead of night to go out on the stoop with his three-year-old brother to watch the bright red northern lights. The grandmother said she knew a war was coming because the northern lights had been red just before the Civil War had begun. The horrors of that war were vaguely sketched in the little boy's mind because of his grandmother's tales of the Shenandoah valley. The potential horror was even clearer since the little boy's father, John Gibson, was in Europe with his

Mother, Augusta Gerloff Hazard, at a German spa. She was born a German and had emigrated to the United States when she was a child but kept her cultural ties with her homeland and returned, now and then, with one of her children to take the waters.

What was now feared was that the war, as it came in August 1914, would close the sea lanes and Grandmother Hazard and John Gibson would not be able to return to the United States. They would be endangered by the U-boats of the Kaiser of Germany.

That earliest of memories is not followed with anything dramatic. Fortunately, the father was able to get through the U-boat blockade and returned to the Solvay Process Company. The company was founded by his great uncle during the latter part of the 19th century after an agreement had been reached with the Solvay family of Belgium to share in developing the soda ash business over the salt wells and lime quarries of Syracuse on the basis of the famous Solvay patented process of production. Many men in the Hazard family left Rhode Island and joined the rest of those who had "moved west" to reap their fortunes. John Gibson who graduated from Yale in 1899, became one of the family team. He soon evidenced executive ability, became Secretary of the company, and the man who had to work out the company's financing with the bankers of New York.

While performing these financing functions during World War I, John Gibson met his death in December 1918. It was not a heroic death on the battlefield. He remained in the factory to see that munitions were produced, first for the Russian Imperial and French armies and later for the Americans. On one of his business trips, he contracted typhoid fever and died of pneumonia just after Christmas 1918. He left his family without a father. The courageous Ada, from the Shenandoah valley with her memories of Civil War hardships, was left alone with her two little sons aged nine and seven and her sixteen-year-old daughter.

No one thought the family could remain in the big house because John Gibson had borrowed heavily to take up his options to purchase Solvay Process stock. But, Ada proved her mettle. She retained a remarkably astute Syracuse lawyer named Charles Andrews, and together they saved the home, paid off the debts, and went on to create a nestegg. When Ada died in 1930, she had created no great fortune but did accumulate enough money to live comfortably.

Yet, Ada was not content to rest on her laurels. She was determined that all three children develop their musical talents to fill those orchestra desks if the world should collapse again as it had in 1865. Every morning, little John Newbold (named for his father's father rather than his father) was hurried down to the piano room at 7 a.m. to practice his violin for one hour. Ada accompanied him on the piano and kept him working even when he felt faint from the effort and had to lie down. For the years from six to twelve, the little boy had that early morning disciplined experience. Looking back upon it, the experience shaped his life. It became second nature to work hard, to accomplish a task that was set, and to stick to a job when it was distasteful and boring. Further, it had other influences: It kept him from joining his playmates at their back lot baseball games, since his lessons on the violin were held twice a week in the cavernous building of Crouse Hall at Syracuse University. Conrad Becker, head of the violin department at the university, had agreed to take on the little boy to pace his own daughter who was of the same age. So, twice a week the boy was driven across town to walk up the hill and to climb the stairs, often against the driving snow of that snow-laden city. He was simply not available to play games. He never became athletic; indeed, he even shunned athletics and had no interest in them even as a spectator sport. He was a thin, wiry, skinny, music major whose life was turned toward discipline on the violin and hard study of homework under similar discipline. That discipline became the major recollection of his childhood.

Another fortuitous event influenced the boy's development: He started in public school at the age of ten. Like most other youngsters of his James Street neighborhood, he had been taken to private schools at the start, first to a Montessori school, then to the Goodyear-Burlingame School which enjoyed the reputation of giving the most rigorous education in the neighborhood. It was a good education, but the school ran out of boys in the upper grades. Ada decided that John Newbold would have to transfer to another school if he were to have contact with fellow boys. She thought the transfer even more important because her husband was dead, and there was no male in the house except his little brother. It was just Ada and Ella Dowding, a most loyal companion present as nurse during John Newbold's birth, and who returned to help Ada as she struggled with her health.

So it was that John Newbold entered the fifth grade at the Lincoln School, where classrooms held fifty children with one teacher who taught all subjects. She would start at the blackboard at one corner of the room and do, over and over again on every slate, the same problem in arithmetic, explaining it all each time. At the last slate she would ask who was left who did not understand. Fortunately for young John, his preceding education had been so good that classes seemed easy, and the teacher suggested he skip a half grade and enter sixth grade next term. This he did, and again after a term he was invited to skip another half grade. This meant that he was a year younger than the other children when he finished eighth grade and graduated from what was then called "grammar school."

In a sense, the experience of skipping was good: It inculcated the sense that learning was easy and that grades were not hard to get if one did homework in a disciplined way. But, it accentuated the sense of separateness, which the early years of a music-oriented boyhood away from the playing fields, had created. Public schools had plenty of big boys who seemed like "tuffies" to the younger ones. There was no defense, except to "disappear," and this young John learned to do. He did not grow up on the fighting mat with those who wanted to test his mettle. He learned to avoid confrontation and to do so— not by absenting himself when things got hot—but by "negotiating" out conflicts before they boiled over. With hindsight, this experience taught him to search for a life in which the negotiator, the lawyer, the peacemaker was to be preferred over that of the militant who sought to settle disputes by a "punch in the nose." That sensitivity to peaceful persuasion was to be brought to his mind many years later, during World War II, when he found himself working in the Lend-Lease office under a retired Major General of the U.S. Army. That old soldier once said that respect could be obtained only by playing "tough." For the thirty-two-year-old before him, however, respect came quite as certainly as peacemaker who tried to achieve his goals by non-belligerent means.

Again, the absence of a father at home was to touch young John when he graduated from grammar school. Most of the students went on to one or the other of Syracuse's noted high schools. Ada thought Syracuse schools would not provide the kind of education or the environment her son needed to prepare himself for the place she hoped he would eventually fill in life. She wanted him to be among men of culture, and she turned to her husband's boyhood preparatory school, The Hill School in Pottstown, Pennsylvania. Off to Pottstown Mother and son went in September 1921. The Headmaster, Dwight Meigs, decided that a Syracuse grammar school education was insufficient preparation for the rigorous curriculum at The Hill. He placed the boy in the second form which meant he would spend five years rather than four years in high school. In truth, there was no repetition: The Headmaster was right. Young John did not even know he was "repeating," because the work load was heavy. He thought that the program was a five year program and would lead to college. He settled down with no sense that he could relax on his oars. His disciplined work pattern brought the success his mother had hoped for: The weekly reports were most often all "A's," and as he looked back upon it only mathematics and Latin were really hard.

The boy's work habits called for early rising, rather than late study. He was up every morning an hour before breakfast. A study room was provided for those like himself. The students had an early morning "club" where they put the finishing touches on the heavy homework program set for the day. Also, he continued his study of the violin with a remarkable elderly teacher named, fondly, Duke Stafford. He saw to it that John worked hard, played in the chapel orchestra, the school orchestra, and occasionally played duets in school shows with a classmate who was better than he. Days were filled with classes, music, and compulsory athletics. It was in the latter that John did not shine. His Syracuse boyhood, in which he ignored athletics, hung over him. Now, he was required to play. This meant that in the fall he had to don a football uniform and play center on the most junior "far fields" team where he was knocked on his seat at every play. He hated it. And, in the winter he had to box a classmate in gym. Again, he hated it and sought to find a teammate who also hated it. He tried to find a teammate willing to play it soft while giving the gym instructor the impression that the play was straight. In the spring it was center field on the far fields, a position where the poor player would cause as little damage as possible because few could hit high flies in that league. But, one memorable occasion is firmly fixed in John's mind: He was standing under a high fly that slipped through his fingers and hit him squarely in the Adam's apple. Although knocked to the ground and hardly able to breathe or swallow, he jumped to his feet, picked up the ball with fear that he would be mercilessly criticized if he did not return it immediately, and threw it as best he could to second base. Athletics were clearly not his forte, but he had to go on throughout the five years.

High scholarship, although not the highest in the school, brought him some honors upon graduation, and off he went to Yale, his father's alma mater. His thoughts at Yale were turned toward international relations and the humanities. Although he had not liked Latin at school, he was told that to earn a B.A. a student must major in Latin. He was also told that a B.A. was far better as an open-sesame to a job, than a B.Ph., which was the "lesser" degree open to humanities majors. So Latin it was but with an equally important emphasis upon history, government and international relations.

The international relations bent had been created from two influences: James Brown Scott and Nicholas J. Spykman. Scott was the brother of his mother Ada's best friends in Syracuse, and he had visited there often. At the Versailles conference Scott had been President Wilson's adviser on international law. He helped found the American Society of International Law, and dominated its activities. He was also

Secretary-General of the Carnegie Endowment for International Peace. Time and again on Syracuse visits, he had told the little boy to head for a career in international law. At Yale, this meant starting with international relations, and it was easy to do, because Yale had one of the pioneers in this discipline, Nicholas J. Spykman. It was to Spykman that the young Eli turned and in whom he found a thrilling master.

But, there was another formative circumstance that turned the young college boy toward international relations: namely, considerable travel experience. Again, this was Ada's doing. In 1924, she put the boy into the hands of a schoolboy study tour of Europe, in which ten groups of boys, each under their own master, set out for a grand tour of Western Europe. Howard Bement of The Hill had his group, which included young John. Off they went to the sights, but not just as tourists. In good Bement fashion everything was explained in its historical and cultural context along the way. Since it was long before the coming of airplanes, there were two long sea voyages, many bus and train trips, and close examination of each country from the ground.

One episode stood out as humiliating and occurred in Rome. His table mates suggested that young John accompany them to the Colosseum: "to see the herd of Papal bulls!" John was pretty sure that the Pope had no herd, but he could imagine that there were some bulls in the Colosseum. His education on church history was totally lacking, so he bit hard on the joke. To this day, he remembers that a poor education can be humiliating, and became determined to learn as much as he could. American history and culture were not enough.

Again, in the summer of 1926, he went back to Europe; this time only to Paris. His companion was the organist of his family's Syracuse church. He studied French every day with an exacting teacher in the shadow of the Sorbonne on Boulevard Saint Michel. He studied violin with M. Laparra, *concertmeister* of the leading symphony orchestra of Paris. Both activities kept him busy, but each evening his companion took him to the Opéra Comique to sit on the first two *strapontins* in the center aisle right behind the conductor. With scores upon their laps the older man and the boy followed the music, until many of that House's repertory operas and ballets became almost memorized: *Carmen, Lakmé, Louise, Tales of Hoffman, Coppélia* and all the rest.

With such early childhood experiences, the die was being cast for a lifetime later spent in international relations and law, and James Brown Scott left his mark. Scott turned up again as a major influence during John's final year at the Harvard Law School. At that time, preparation was under way to become a practicing lawyer in Syracuse after his LL.B.

had been earned, but in April of his third year he was in for quite a surprise. It was in Manley O. Hudson's class, Harvard's famous professor of international law, and later Judge on the International Court of Justice. John was in that class seemingly by chance, but it was not really chance, for Scott's influence had to do with it.

What happened was this: In picking out courses for a third year, it seemed that for Scott's sake, international law should be included among the thoroughly bread-and-butter courses. There was no expectation that international law would help a practice in Syracuse, but Scott had said that the subject was worthwhile. The young man had tried to obtain an introduction to international law while still an undergraduate at Yale. In his junior year he had called upon the famous Professor Edwin Borchard at the Law School and asked if he might attend his class during the senior year. Borchard said yes, and that he should come around for a signature just before spring term 1930. When the senior appeared in Borchard's office as requested, he was told that the class had been given in fall 1929, and they had forgotten to tell the applicant of the change. That being so, no international law had been studied at Yale, and Hudson's course at Harvard looked like a second opportunity.

It turned out to be the turning point in his life: In April 1934, Hudson asked young John Hazard and a colleague to follow him to his office after class. Hudson was a man of few words. When the two students reached his office, he turned around and said simply: "I have a request to nominate a student to study law in Russia for three years. Would either of you like to do it?" Hazard stood silently for a moment, but his comrade spoke up immediately and said he had his job already arranged in San Francisco. He was also engaged to be married, and under the circumstances the opportunity did not interest him.

Hazard asked for the weekend to think about it. He telephoned James Brown Scott in Washington and asked if he might come down to see him. He took the train and rode the long trip from Boston to Washington. Scott received him like a loving uncle, heard of Hudson's proposal, and said one simple thing: "If you can begin at an early age to specialize in international law, do so. I had to wait until I was in my thirties."

No one knew what the study of law in Russia would be like. The United States had recognized the U.S.S.R. after years of hostility in the autumn of 1933. Roosevelt hoped that recognition would lead to increased trade, and that this would serve as a stimulus to lift the United States out of the Great Depression. The Hudson proposal had been based upon a request of a New York foundation, the Institute of Current

World Affairs, which had courted the Russian Information Office during the later years of non-recognition hoping to gain access for students in Russia when recognition finally occurred. When it did arrive, the Institute's director, Walter S. Rogers, asked Boris Skvirsky, the Information Office's director, to bring in an answer. When it arrived, Rogers approached Hudson, and that led to the proposal.

Hazard was well aware of the risks in going to a revolutionary country which he had seen in 1930 during the first leg of a trip around the world with three Yale classmates. At that time, he had decided Russia was a hopelessly poor, disorganized and undisciplined country. He even wrote his sister that he never wanted to see it again, and now here he was considering a three-year assignment in Moscow. The decision was not easy. He saw two more of his favorite Harvard professors. Both encouraged him to accept, and by Monday morning he was ready to tell Hudson that he would accept the nomination. It went through the Board of the Institute of Current World Affairs, and after several interviews with forbidding Board members, the most frightening of whom was Henry Allen Moe the world-famous director of the Guggenheim Foundation, and by August 1934 the young hopeful Hazard was on his way. He knew no Russian, no Russian history and no Marxist theory. He knew only that a career of uniqueness might result, and that was reason enough to risk going into a strange country. Most of his fellow Harvard classmates told him he would have difficulty escalating to a partnership in a firm in New York, and might end up without a job.

A final word may be appropriate about that trip around the world in academic year 1930-31 upon graduation from Yale. Hazard planned it with three friends all of whom saw the depression looming, and who had all developed a real interest in far horizons. The trip was planned step-by-step as the quartet traveled along. They stuck to land travel wherever possible and began in Russia at Leningrad. They visited the construction site of the Ford Factory at Nizhni Novgorod, and then Moscow, Kiev and Odessa, went south to Turkey, Greece and Egypt, and then overland through Jerusalem, Damascus, Baghdad, Teheran, the desert of Baluchistan to India. The group traveled from Calcutta to Burma by ship. From Rangoon it was overland again, up the Irrawady River to the back door of China, across the Shan states of Burma on what was to become the Burma Road in the Second World War, out through Siam and Cambodia to Saigon, by ship to Singapore and on to Indonesia, the Philippines and Hong Kong, then into Canton and up the coast to Shanghai followed by overland train to Peking, Mukden, Korea and across the ferry to Japan. Nine months of study travel at the level of "third class" was an eye opener, and an appetite creator. It was to influence that final judgment to go to Russia, for although Russia itself looked undesirable, the world looked very important, and the Soviet experience seemed to be the open-sesame to a career in the world. Indeed, it turned out to be so, for Soviet law, although of utility in its narrow professional sense, has led its practitioner to many lands as lecturer, visiting professor and student of socialist systems.

In retrospect, each step that seemed so unplanned as it was taken, turned out instead to look like a planned prologue. Some time was wasted, undoubtedly, along the way, but enough proved to be useful in development of a career. The impression has remained that whatever one does in life, there will come a moment when all life's experiences will be useful.

Chapter One
AROUND THE WORLD

AROUND THE WORLD

The most influential winter of Hazard's young life began with tragedy. During the last week of August 1930, his Mother died. She had been as vivacious as ever the night before while the family talked of the young man's impending trip around the world. The next morning the blow struck, and in a few days it was over. The question was: Could the trip continue? The lawyers said it would take a year to settle Ada's estate, and there was no reason for Hazard to remain in America. The other family members urged Hazard to go ahead and he did. Within days, he was off to New York to board the freighter that was to take him and his three Yale classmates, Thomas Moore, John Musser, and Arthur Palmer, to Helsinki.

Hazard had crossed the Atlantic before but on passenger liners. This was a slow freighter of the American Scantic Line. A handful of passengers ate their meals with the officers and dallied for hours as the old salts told of wild escapades and of serious business problems in running a merchant ship. There were brief stops at Copenhagen and Stockholm, and finally the ship reached her goal. Off the four young men went to the Soviet Consulate to get visas. Because the United States had not yet recognized the Bolsheviks, visas had to be obtained abroad, but arrangements had been made through a travel company in New York that acted as a go-between.

The Soviet Consulate was Hazard's first glimpse of Russians. When the door opened on the red carpets of the old mansion, an air of mystery, which he was to come to know well when he became a student in Moscow many years later, pervaded the place. Little windows in walls were opened to see the newcomers. Voices were hushed. One had the sense of being looked over very carefully. But the visas were there, and after a few days, the quartet went on the border train. The last stop in Finland was a model of cleanliness and good order and with plenty of food. The first stop on the other side, however, was pandemonium: It was unkempt, noisy, unclean, and pervaded, again, by mystery as border guards scanned the visas and the passengers. One would think the passengers were entering to undo the revolution. It was a first glimpse of what was to become routine.

Leningrad had its palaces, but its squalor was pathetic although grand. Paint was peeling off buildings; people looked threadbare. Moscow was even more foreboding, and there was the tragic moment outside the old Grand Hotel when the quartet found the body of a starved boy lying in the gutter. A train ride took the group to Nizhni-Novgorod where the Austin Company of Cleveland was building the Soviet Union's first automobile plant. Again, the impression, conveyed with confirmation by the American engineers, was that there was no discipline because foremen dared not prod their charges. A five minute smoking break was allowed each hour, but no one was allowed to take five minutes at the same time. Dormitories were being built to house parents and children, but not as a housekeeping unit. Communism of that era seemed to require the families to eat in a dining hall below. Only a few housekeeping units were being built as experiments.

Kiev with its famous Lavra was Russia, or rather the Ukraine, as Americans like to think of it: gold domes, bell towers, monasteries. But, again there were signs of the new era—mostly in the attention given to children at the crèches. Finally, there came Odessa, a real ruin. The quartet stayed at the famous old Hotel de Londres which overlooked the splendid harbor but was run down to the level of fourth class in the West. Then came the task of getting out of the country. Here again there was the tussle with bureaucracy before the Italian ship for Istanbul could be boarded. Every document had to be checked and rechecked, and unhurriedly. When the Odessa harbor faded away, the quartet concluded that they had seen enough of communism, and doubted that it had a brilliant future.

After many days at sea, their adventures in the Islamic World began, as the ship sailed through the Bosphorus. At this point, the quartet felt themselves back in the "West" by comparison. Of course, there were minarets and the smells of the East, but they were put up at Robert College, which was, at the time, an American run institution where friends took time out of busy schedules to show the sights and explain the history of the Second Rome, and the coming of the Moslems. It was dramatic: A history hardly taught at all in the American colleges where Byzantium is, or, at least used to be, ignored.

Although a brief visit to Athens intervened on the trip south to Alexandria, the group was soon among the Arabs. Years later, Hazard gave a ready answer to the question: "Why are you so happy?" His stock reply was: "I have seen the Arab World." This meant that the Arab world was so impoverished and so sad that anything in the "West," no matter how grim, looked like paradise. Oil had not yet become a factor to the Arabs, and education was only beginning to modernize them. One element in this modernization program was observed along the quartet's route. They began with the American University in Cairo where the genial Dr. Charles Watson, its President, and a friend of one of the quartet saw to it that they understood Cairo, past and present. Still, there was no cause for rejoicing in what was happening. It was a long slow process to raise the level of Cairo even to the slums of New York.

From Cairo, the trip East began: The train crossed the Suez Canal to Palestine, dropped the men off in Jerusalem where the Vice-Consul of the United States, Ned Blatchford, with a lifetime of experience, gave them a sense of the history of the Holy places and of the Arab-Jewish conflict. Hazard got an impression that has stayed with him ever since: There will never be a solution to the conflict. It is the meeting of two unbending wills.

From Jerusalem and the Holy Land, it was north to Damascus, and across the desert tract to Baghdad. The picture of the long trails of dust rising behind the old cars as they sped across the sands, broken only by a glass of tea at a midway adobe inn in the middle of the night, remains forever. By morning the car was passing the Great Mosque with its golden towers and domes, the epitome of the American's idea of the Islamic world. Some days the men rested at the YMCA in Baghdad. Their next stage was to be the most exhausting one. They crossed what was then Persia, a country awakening from its long sleep under the first of the Pahlevis.

Again, it was the intimate glimpses at the various American Missions along the way, and St. George's College in Teheran, where a Yale graduate of a year earlier was a teacher. Persians were forbidden to wear the fez. In its place a cake box hat with a visor which looked odd to Western eyes was substituted. The villages with their adobe houses looked as poor as anything seen in Egypt. The endless desert, the high mountains, the bitter cold of October nights, the long daily rides in the car that had been rented with driver and tire changer, were hectic because the driver suffered from malaria and had alternating fits of fevers and shivers. One of the quartet took over most of the driving. Finally, diarrhea struck Hazard, so heavily that it seemed amoebic. There was nothing to do but go on. Nights spent on the board beds of camel stops or on the floors of adobe houses did not help. But, youth saved the day. It was still possible to travel, despite all their problems, and to marvel at the ancient historic sights, especially Meshed, which seemed to the travelers like the outpost of the world.

One incident gave the flavor of the monarchy. One morning, as the car bumped along over the desert roads, the driver was called off to the side. None of the quartet could understand why the group had to wait, but it was clearly important. The village garrison was out practicing simple drills in anticipation of the Shah's arrival. It was ludicrous to eyes that had seen palace guards in the European capitals, but also touching, for the men in their baggy uniforms were trying hard. As the little group waited by the roadside close by the garrison, a dust cloud appeared on the horizon and sped closer. At last the car careened along the rutted road and tore past the little garrison waiting to do its act. In the back seat sat the Shah, asleep, giving no recognition, even by a wave of his hand, to his subjects who had wanted to do him honor. In a moment it was over. The car was out of sight, and the moment of a lifetime for those villagers had passed. The westerners marveled at the opportunity that had been missed for some good public relations, but evidently the Shah felt no need for public acclaim. He seemed out of touch with his people. Perhaps his son's upbringing was to make the disaster of fifty years later inevitable.

The road ended at the railhead of Duzdap (Zahidan) to which the Indian railways ran in Persia. For Hazard it was his mecca. An Indian innkeeper, when told of Hazard's malady said: "I have just the medicine for you Sahib." Hazard was put to bed with a bottle of peregoric, and in the morning his diarrhea had stopped. The quartet, miraculously, was ready to take the long trip across the Baluchistan desert to what was not yet a divided Pakistan and India. The first stop was Lahore where a former classmate was teaching in Forman Christian College. The quartet settled down for a few days in a college environment that seemed like home after what they had gone through. India was also poor, but it seemed more hopeful than the Arab world—at least, on first impression.

The quartet got its first impression of the conflict between British masters and the great numbers of educated Indian youths who envied their masters' jobs. The quartet traveled long journeys in what was then called intermediate class, a step between the overly crowded third class, filled with the peasants and their bags; and the respectable second class, occupied by the lower levels of the civil service, and the bourgeoisie. Its passengers were the highly vocal young men who had been educated in London; who knew their history and their classics, but who had returned to India to fill jobs that were not commensurate with their newly acquired knowledge. They talked endlessly during the long nights on the train of the oppression of the British *raj*.

In contrast there were the young men from Oxford and Cambridge who were met in the YMCA's of the big cities who had prepared themselves to govern and to stay until they could retire, eventually, to a thatched cottage in Devon with a good pension. When asked when India would be self-governing, their answer was simple: in 500 years! To them, the country was simply too chaotic, too inefficient, too divided between religions and castes ever to become a viable governing unit. It needed England and its civil servants to make it work. The grand buildings of New Delhi were seen as the promise of what the *raj* could do. The slums of Calcutta were nothing like those of the present day but were bad enough to Western eyes. They were a measure of the distance yet to go.

Of course, there followed the glimpses of Everest from Darjeeling, the incredible heights of the mountains pushing into the purple and blue haze; the reflections on Dal Lake high in the mountains of Kashmir where the quartet did the British thing and stayed on a houseboat for one week with a bearer to care for their every wish; the stately palaces of the Maharajas; and the tombs, including the most ethereal of all, the Taj Mahal. This was the beautiful India of the picture books, but along with it went the people who swarmed around, who gathered at trainsides when the quartet arrived to fight with each other for what little commission they might earn from an innkeeper whom they represented when foreigners arrived.

From Calcutta, they went by ship to Rangoon where a surprise awaited. At the Baptist Mission, the quartet met Harold Young and his family at their first dinner. Harold told them he had been born in Burma into a missionary family and was assigned to a mission just over the Chinese border from the Shan states of Burma. Young was about to return to his remote outpost when he finished his annual purchasing trip to Rangoon. The quartet pleaded with him to let them go along, and he agreed. Their expenses were set at one rupee a day which was equivalent at the time to twenty-five cents. The quartet agreed to meet him a week or so later at the railhead upcountry. Meanwhile they would take the river boat up to Mandalay, stay a few days in January of 1931 with the Colonel who had been Hazard's cousin's commanding officer during years in the British Army in India, and then go on by rail to Hsipau.

At the appointed place and time, the quartet arrived to find Harold testing mountain ponies in the open market. Harold planned to buy the ponies for the quartet to ride across the mountains and jungles into China. When this was done, the pack ponies, the pack oxen, the quartet and the mission family—with its two little children—started off across the paddy fields into the woods. The bearers from Harold's various Christian settlements also went with them. It was a caravan, which passed by the often morose hill people with their spears and simple G-strings, with an occasional skin as cape. Some nights would be spent sleeping in temples under the eyes of the golden Buddhas. Local princes would sell them rice and greet them with pomp. The quartet bought some German-made artificial rubies and sapphires in Rangoon to give as gifts. Harold thought them excellent for the purpose, although fakes.

Finally, the frontier was reached. They had their first encounter with Chinese bureaucracy thousands of miles southwest of Nanking. Harold told his family and the quartet to remain out of sight with the caravan animals until he had talked with the Chinese commissioner across the little river that was the frontier. He said it might take quite a time: He would have to sip tea, chat about life in general, and finally get around to the fact that he had in tow four young Americans who were to be his guests at the mission for a short spell. Of course, the Chinese could be suspicious, and, of course, the official would have no way of communicating with Nanking. He would have to take the personal risk of letting some dangerous types into China.

All went well. The caravan animals forded the stream, and the humans were ferried across in rustic boats. On the bank, they met the owner of a tea caravan who sat on his haunches to exchange British Indian rupees for Chinese dragon silver dollars. Each was bounced off a rock to be sure that it gave the ring of genuineness, and the deal was closed.

The Bana Mission in Yunnan Province of China was an eye-opener, since Harold had been very successful in converting the people of the neighborhood. Each had been taught that Christians shake hands, so at every stop along the trail the village turned out, and every last villager, down to the youngest babe on the back, had to have his hand shaken by each of the strange guests. By that time the group was being called "the four white majesties." Two of them had reputations as miracle men because en route across Burma they swam the mighty Salween river as it roared south from the snowfields of the Himalayas to the sea. This seemed like a crazy adventure to the two quartet members who refused even to think of it, but one of the men had been a three-letter man at Yale who felt ready for any physical test, and the other had been a strong swimmer.

These two jumped into the icy water, and were immediately carried way down the river by its swift current. One has since confided, after fifty years, that he thought it was to be his last swim. But, they got across a river which was such a mighty spirit that, in the minds of the hill peoples, it calmed the wildest of horses as they were ferried across on planks stretched across dugout canoes. With such a reputation, which spread like wildfire over the distances of the mountain people, their reception at Bana was assured. People came from miles around to see these wonder-men, and they put on their traditional dances for the guests.

The time came, alas, to move on. Harold said he would take the quartet back to Burma and find a caravan going south to Siam across the Shan states. He had proved to be an engaging, even thrilling man, and the parting was sad. Hazard's final words were: "Harold, if there is another great war you will not know it, for you are so far away." That sentence was to stick in Hazard's memory. When the awful day of the Second

World War came, he remembered it, for General Stillwell opened that very trail as the famous Burma Road from Burma to China, and his principal interpreter, among the hill people, was none other than the same Harold Young!

A lead caravan guided by its Chinese owners took the quartet south to the Burmese-Siamese border without incident, although the group was never sure that they would not meet the noted bandits of the area, or even be led astray by their guides and robbed or murdered. Hazard had a good Survey map of India, showing every trail among the contours. He scrutinized every crossing to see whether it looked like the right path. On one occasion, when he opened the map while on horseback, his horse was startled by the flash of white behind his ears and bolted down the trail. Hazard clasped his feet together and slowly slipped under the horse's belly, because he had taken his feet from the stirrups. Finally, he let go and to this day remembers the pounding horse's hoofs wondering whether they would give him a fatal blow. He walked the rest of the way to the frontier.

Siam, as Thailand was then called, was reached by traveling from the Burmese frontier by railroad. A narrow, paved road provided the link to the Burmese trail which ended at a Roman Catholic mission. The Italian priest was overjoyed to see the quartet. All his life the priest had studied English but never actually heard it spoken. For an evening, he spoke as fast as he could and listened to acquire the accents of the Americans. He represented to the quartet complete unselfishness. He told them how he had dreamed of Italy and subscribed to an Italian newspaper but had finally given up, realizing that he could never return, so the sooner he made himself a part of his new home the better.

In Siam, the men were lionized. They had a letter to the King's Uncle, Prince Swasti, who had studied at Oxford. He thought the trip from Burma to China fantastic, and the visit to northern Siam unusual. The prince gave them a banquet, had the Royal dance troupe put on its historic performance, introduced them to the foreign colony, and gave them a sense that they had done something far more important than they thought it themselves. By the time the group had reached Siam they had come to believe anything they heard about the wonders of the East. They were told of fish who flopped across roads from one canal to another to improve their water conditions, of fighting fish trained to battle to the death, and of much else. Hazard remembered his foolish expectation that the Colosseum of Rome might have a herd of bulls. Now he was prepared to be gullible about anything he was told because the world had proved itself so full of incredible things.

The quartet pushed on to the Cambodian frontier to see Angkor Wat.

The last outpost of Siam was an inn managed by a White Russian emigré and his wife. During the night of their stay, the group was awakened by the shrieks of the wife as her husband chased her around the circular porch of the inn with a knife. But, she was there in the morning. It was one more reminder that life was not all roses.

A car took the quartet to Angkor, across the Mekong through Pnom Penh, and on to Saigon. France was everywhere in sight, beginning with the arrogant French border officer. Hazard had come to love France as a result of his various trips and especially his summer of violin and French. Here was a new type of Frenchman: the colonial officer. In the demeanor of one man, it became evident what corruption of character a colonial role can cause—even worse than that of the British officers in India who seemed more like benevolent uncles guiding their nephews along an endless road to maturity. More colonialism was seen in Indonesia where the Dutch held sway and in the Philippines with the Americans. In each, there seemed to be no expectation that the white man could lay down his burden.

To these American young men the Philippines was the most revealing. Here they saw their own people as colonial masters. To be sure, the officials seemed to be running an efficient government, and to be educating the local people as the Dutch would not in their Indonesia. Still there was a sentiment hardly present back in the United States. When one acquaintance, met at the YMCA was asked about the possibilities of independence, he replied: "These people cannot govern themselves. They are divided between the plains and the mountain peoples. They cannot work together. The plains people will take power and exploit their brothers in the mountains mercilessly. Further, there will be wide corruption." While no American spoke of the 500 years the British were using for their period of guardianship, there was the same sense that America would have to remain a long time. When Hazard asked an educated Filipino what he thought of the need for continuing tutelage, he replied: "We want the right to misgovern ourselves." On various return visits to Manila, where the problems of government are all too evident, that farewell comment has rushed through Hazard's memory. Perhaps "misgovernment" is to be preferred to bondage.

China was the treat the quartet had expected. They started at Hong Kong, having crossed from Manila just over the propellers of the Canadian Pacific's prize liner, the Empress of Japan. It was a horribly seasick night, but the lights of Hong Kong revived their spirits. Again, it was the famous Kowloon YMCA which still receives guests in the best deal for the money the Crown Colony affords. Canton was the starter, along with a Yale friend at the University who initiated the quartet. A return visit fifty years later to the same campus proved that with all the changes, some things remain pretty much the same. Canton was hopeful, or at least its foreign educators were hopeful. It was a moment in that spring of 1931 when war lordism was at an ebb. Railroads were back in working order throughout the whole country. There was some political unity directed from Nanking. The government was in the hands of the people, many of whom had been educated in America, and some even at Yale. The tide of the civil war had passed. No communists seemed menacing, as yet, and the Japanese had not arrived. Perhaps China had, at long last, a chance to develop a foreign and domestic peace. The little group was to see a lot of it, because after Canton they sailed up the coast to Shanghai, visited a former Yale professor now at a Mission in Nanking, had a memorable dinner with the top government people who had gone to Yale, then passed on by rail to Peking.

Peking was the gem the group expected. They stayed at the North China Language Institute run by Dr. Pettus who was the father of one of the the quartet's Yale classmates. Their letter of introduction to Mme. Wellington Koo brought invitations to attend her frequent soirées where the intellectuals of the city met in the afternoons to drink and gossip. The young men of the quartet became the show pieces of the month, and many came to see them as something new on the scene. Sandwiched in between visits to the Great Wall, the Forbidden City, the Temple of Heaven, and the endless walks through the fascinating streets with their wedding and funeral processions, the soirées gave a glimpse of the life of the élite and a chance to learn their views of China's future. They also were optimistic. At last the Koumintang was getting things sorted out, and it had good people to guide it.

Still, the quartet could see the poverty of China: the beggars, the hovels, the relics of the past with the bound feet of the defunct Empire. There were those who bemoaned the fact that there were no great natural resources. At the time, no one imagined there would be discoveries of oil and minerals that would make China an industrial giant. It was a land of contrast on the threshhold of what might be a new beginning, but no one could be sure.

From Peking, it was the long train ride through Manchuria to Korea which was still under Japanese domination. Again, missionaries guided the quartet and influenced their thinking. The beauties were self-evident, notably the Diamond Mountains through which the quartet trudged with their backpacks. It looked like a scene from a Chinese painting with little monasteries high on the rugged cliffs often hidden by mist from the trail below. What the people were thinking, the group could not tell. Language barriers cut off conversation as had not been the case in

English-speaking Manila. So, it was with a sense of beauty, of exotic scenes, that the party went south to cross into Japan.

Again, it was exotic beauty that caught the eye. Japan was awakening fast. It was becoming militant. Its eyes were on the raw materials of its neighbors, and the feeling seemed to be that the time must come when they would have to be under Japanese control. But, perhaps this impression is a result of hindsight considering the history of the Japanese military's effort to create the "co-prosperity sphere" in the following decade. Japan was by no means a rich country at this time, nor one that yet had the reputation for innovative production good enough to challenge the industrial giants of the Western world. Distinguished western-trained scholars were good to the travelers; they told them of the history, of the westernization that had occurred since the Meiji restoration, and of the expectations for the future. That future, however, seemed still far from what it has turned out to be in the post-World War II era. Indeed, it never entered the heads of the travelers that Japan would become one of the most important industrial powers in the world.

There remained only the long voyage across the Pacific on a Japanese liner with a stop-over in Honolulu. The travelers were in third class. The bunks were so narrow one could not turn over. The food seemed like cooked-over second class food and the company was, except for eight Europeans, entirely Chinese or Japanese, none of whom were intellectuals. Hawaii was a happy interlude with a first class dinner at the Royal Hawaiian Hotel where the entrance of those swinging hoola girls with their songs and musical instruments seemed like the arrival of angels from paradise. There was even a late night swim on the beach under the Pali. As yet, the Islands had not been overrun with tourists: It was the dreamland that Robert Louis Stevenson had sought out and all that had been expected.

Finally, the Golden Gate, with no bridge yet dreamed of, and the trip was over. Nine months in travel, the equivalent of an academic year, and yet it had crowded in a set of experiences and a host of ideas which went way beyond what the Yale days had taught. This was not to say that the Yale days were not preparation for observation. They were the main courses of the dinner, for which the round-the-world trip was the dessert, and the dessert left the last taste.

A few thoughts became paramount. There were problems in the world that seemed insoluble: Arabs and Jews, Hindus and Moslems, poverty in the face of inadequate resources, the determination of the colonial powers to continue to bear their governing burdens. Yet, on the other hand, there was the evident success of education in creating skills, the beginning of enrichment as the result of industrial development, and, perhaps, best of all, the pride of peoples in their heritage. Poor as they were the Egyptians had once been a great people, and the Persians had created Persepolis. The one gloomy spot was Russia and its communist inefficiency and even brutality. Little did Hazard realize at the time, that it would be to Russia that he would return, and that his life would be devoted to the study of the communist movement.

Chapter Two
MOSCOW STUDENT DAYS

MOSCOW STUDENT DAYS

Adolf Hitler's shadow was cast across Hazard's route to Leningrad in August of 1934. The brief visit in Nazi Germany was unexpected. It came about because the old ship S.S. Aleksei Rykov broke down in the Kiel Canal en route from London to Leningrad, and the layover at Kiel was required to put the motors in order. The Nazis agreed to let the passengers visit the town, and Hazard disembarked with the others. The first stop was the bank to exchange money, and the clerk provided the introduction to the new order. On pushing the marks over the bank counter, he stepped back, raised his arm in the straight arm salute of the Nazis and shouted: "Heil Hitler."

The next incident occurred a few hours later, and it took on added meaning when related to the German obligation assumed at Versailles in 1918 not to rearm. A brigade of men clothed in brown work clothes passed by in perfect military formation carrying shovels instead of guns. They were obviously being trained to march like soldiers. In the afternoon shooting was heard over the hill to the north of the canal. Some of the passengers crossed the bridge to investigate, and saw a shooting range with men practicing. Clearly Hitler was preparing for war.

The Soviets were aware of the danger. When the ship finally set out again, the radio carried the news of the Soviet Union's decision to enter the League of Nations in the face of the growing Nazi menace. What a surprise this was to those who knew of Stalin's rejection of the League as a capitalist cabal set upon destroying communism!

With this cloud upon the horizon, the party reached Leningrad. It was already gloomy, rainy, and cold as Northern Europe always is when autumn advances. Hazard set out immediately for Moscow which he remembered as the scene of inefficiency, poverty, and the starvation of the little boy in the gutter in front of the hotel. Times had changed, however, and things looked better even though it was still far from the promised comfortable society. Public buildings were not yet heated. Supplies were scarce. Foreign currency stores picked up what they could from foreigners and citizens who could pay with marks, francs, dollars or gold.

Hazard was lucky and found a room. He remained in a hotel only a few days since the United States Lines representative, a former room mate of Adolph Berle at Harvard to whom he turned upon his arrival, said he had a place for him. It was a room with a family where the representative had lived until he married a Russian woman a short time previously. Hazard was introduced to Marta Abramovna Krasnushkina, who was to be his foster mother for the rest of his stay in Moscow. She was a doctor of a prominent Jewish family sent to Germany before the Revolution to be trained. Upon her return, she married a prominent psychiatrist, Evgenii Konstantinovich. They had been able to save some money from the difficult years during the period of war communism and had qualified for the lease of a house during the period of the New Economic Policy because they had agreed to put it into repair. Consequently, they were not subject to the limits on subleasing which applied in government-owned buildings, and they had a room they leased to the United States Lines representative for foreign currency which they could use in the *Torgsin* stores. Hazard moved in and found that the family included a son who was a Ph.D. student in physics and a daughter who was a student actress at the famous Stanislavsky acting school. This was his family: an educated sophisticated group that found a way to survive under the new regime. Not until many years later did Hazard learn that the father had become a psychiatrist-consultant to the security police, the G.P.U., and Marta Abramovna was his contact.

Evgenii Konstantinovich had nothing to do with Hazard. He ate at different hours from the rest of the family. He never even joined the rest of the family for the traditional big dinner of the Russians at 3 p.m. He grunted in recognition when he met Hazard in the corridor. He appeared to be a morose man. Marta Abramovna was quite the reverse, however. She treated Hazard as a son, coming into his little room to chat about anything. On one occasion she had in hand a form with Hazard's photograph upon it. She said it was the police questionnaire. She asked what she should put on the sheet about Hazard's activities, his contacts, his conversations.

The Russian language was his number one task. Hazard had taken a few Berlitz lessons in conversation before departure from New York, but he could only say a few simple things. The friend who suggested the apartment suggested a teacher, Bella Isaevna Liberman. Bella had fled, with her father, to America after the revolution of 1905 and had learned perfect American English. Upon her return after the 1917 revolution, she had exploited her knowledge and in 1934 was teaching English in the Institute of the People's Commissariat of Foreign Trade. She agreed to come to Hazard's little room for an hour every day for the first month, and, after that, every other day for two hours he would be received at her apartment. Russian is hard, and it took seven hours to prepare for the one hour sessions. She took a child's grammar used in the Soviet schools and set Hazard off on a course of learning Russian as if he were a first grade student. Then he read editorials in the children's newspaper *Pionerskaia Pravda*, and moved slowly up to the adult leagues of *Izvestiia* and *Pravda*. His family helped with conversation, although at the outset Marta Abramovna spoke French when she communicated with him.

Law School sessions did not begin for Hazard until the second semester in February 1935, but contact was made immediately with the Professor of International Law to whom Hazard had a letter from Professor Manley Hudson of Harvard. The professor was world famous as the first author in the U.S.S.R. on international law. He took the position that the U.S.S.R. used conventional international law to protect itself, but, in so doing, created a new law of the transitional period from capitalism to communism. His book on the topic, published under his name Evgenii Aleksandrovich Korovin in 1924, had been studied around the world. He was an old timer, who spoke flawless French. He made his peace with the Bolsheviks although he was not a Party member at that time, and he professed to be an enthusiast. At the very end of Hazard's three years, he said when he parted: "Ivan Ivanovich, we are doing with communism what the Christians have tried unsuccessfully to do for centuries." He saw communism as a humanistic approach. It lacked at the moment, perfection, contained some terrible blemishes, but held extraordinary promise. He was not afraid to be innovative in his books and articles, but stayed always within what he conceived to be a Marxist framework.

Korovin agreed to receive Hazard twice a month to talk about his progress and his questions. They would speak French until Hazard's Russian was up to serious conversation. Those evening discussions were the most memorable part of the three years. To make them worth something to his host, Hazard abstracted articles in the *American Journal of International Law* and Western books about Soviet law. He used these abstracts as notes for the conversation. He even persuaded Korovin to write a review of the then popular book on Soviet international law by T.A. Taracouzio, a researcher at the Harvard Law School.

Classes began in February 1935 as the new semester opened. Hazard had seen Dean Sakach, a Party representative without any known legal background. His Vice-Dean was F.I. Kozhevnikov, later to be elected to the International Court of Justice in The Hague, and a recognized scholar. Hazard's Russian was still poor, but he entered the big lecture hall of the Moscow Institute of Soviet Law. Over the podium hung a great sketch of Stalin in the place occupied before the revolution by a mosaic of Christ in what had been the hall of worship in the Seminary. Hazard placed his dictionary on his lap and the magisterial type lecture began.

As there was no heat in the building, students and professors wore their street coats and fur hats. The clerestory windows in the high ceilinged rooms were kept open to reduce the humidity from human breath. Crows flew in through these windows, circled the rooms flapping their wings. There was no discipline among the students. They sailed paper airplanes toward the professor as he spoke and tried not to hit him. A year later a decree ordered students to maintain discipline in classrooms, and ordered the grammar school children to salute their teachers. Clearly, Soviet youth was in the undisciplined state Hazard had observed on his trip to the new Ford plant in Nizhni Novgorod in 1930.

At the first intermission the students gathered around to see this new curiosity. They asked Hazard to show his hands and said to each other: "He is not a worker." His hands told the story, for there were no calluses. Still, they were friendly. Many wore a uniform of sorts, but most were in ordinary worker's baggy clothes. It was a coeducational faculty, and there were many women students. Fortunately, every course had a set of mimeographed lecture notes, along with printed textbooks. He used these with his teacher in the late afternoon sessions at her apartment to learn the precise vocabulary necessary to understand the course. Consequently, he learned a legal vocabulary. In spite of her efforts to get him to memorize Pushkin and Lermontov, Hazard never developed a vocabulary suited to *belles lettres*.

The topics were not difficult. Students asked how he grasped them quickly. The answer was simple: In spite of all of the talk about a "new law," the general terms and concepts bore some relation to law in the West. There were contracts, torts, crimes, family relations, and court procedure, just as there had been at Harvard. What was new was the emphasis upon Marxism and its impact on legal theory and practice. There was the law relating to state production enterprises and collective farms. There was the theory to be learned that a labor contract was a partnership in production between state management and working man and not a means of "exploitation." It was not hard to memorize the lines like an actor and to repeat them on the oral examinations which followed at the end of each term. The first question on these examinations was always "Compare the bourgeois and Soviet law" on whatever topic was the subject of the course. What was hard was the Russian language in which the answer had to be given, not the substantive law. Hazard recalled the first examination in civil law, the key subject in any

Continental European law faculty. He felt beforehand like Christ at Gethsemane. He wanted to have the cup pass from him.

The examination was in the usual form: Students entered the classroom at the appointed hour, drew a paper out of a bowl, read the questions and sat in a corner to prepare while others recited. Then came the frightening moment. The student was called forward before a bench of three: the magisterial lecturer in the course; his assistant, the *dotsent;* and a graduate student, the *aspirant*. The recitation would begin. Interruptions followed from the bench, and for Hazard the emphasis was always on comparison with bourgeois law. At the end of the twenty minutes or so, the bench would confer, take the student's examination book, enter a grade, and the professor would then sign. For civil law, the professor was the renowned Amfiteatrov. He was later removed from his position during the Great Purge of 1937 for having been close to E.B. Pashukanis and, therefore, in favor of withering away the civil law to put in its place a new economic law designed to facilitate relationships between state productive enterprises performing under the compulsory state economic plan.

At the end of the ordeal, Amfiteatrov wrote in the book: "khorosho," which would be the approximate equivalent of a "B" in America. He smiled and so did the dotsent, but the aspirant blurted out: "Tovarishch Khazard, you know the subject, but your language is terrible." He was right. The Russian language is very difficult.

The most fascinating lectures were those of the internationalists, Korovin in international public law, and I.S. Pereterski in international private law. Both were highly cultured scholars of the old school. They filled their lectures with anecdotes from history and comments of the great body of law developed by the bourgeois states. Although Korovin spoke with impeccable Russian, Pereterski tended to swallow his words, and it was not so easy to follow. The most difficult lectures were in theory of state and law and political economy. This material was all new to Hazard. He had to read the Marxist classics. Fortunately some were in English within the foreign community, and he would borrow the translation for a weekend and concentrate on it. He recalls one heavy weekend with Engels' *Origin of the Family, Private Property, and the State*.

Hazard supplemented the theoretical material at the Law Institute with what he could pick up at an English language class at the Foreign Workers Club. It was at the club that he studied the history of the Communist Party and dialectical materialism. His teacher at the club was a hard-bitten Hungarian communist who regaled the group after class at the milk bar with stories of how he had hidden out in barns when he tried to foment trouble in America some years earlier.

Entrance into the Club was not easy; the membership committee feared penetration by spies. There were sections for each linguistic group of members: German, Polish, French, Spanish, and, of course, English. The English group comprised: Australians, Americans, Canadians and all others who used English as a language. Hazard had not come as a foreign worker. He was a student, and he retained his links with the United States Embassy and refrained from giving noisy support to the current policy of Stalin. How was he to gain admittance? The president of the English language section was an American who was said to have once been the Communist Party candidate for governor of Connecticut. Hazard was admitted through a quiet American who worked for the Soviet photo enterprise which sent news photos abroad and also translated Russian poetry into English. They were about the same age, and each had respect for the other. Each knew on which side of the barricade the other stood, but they had learned the value of coexistence in personal relationships. As a result, Hazard had his sponsor and was admitted into the Club

Membership in the Club offered an opportunity. Hazard came to know the committed staff of English-speaking members of the Comintern. He heard the Australian tell of his role at the famous battle of Gallipoli; he heard the Englishmen tell of their work in British factories to spread the Marxist gospel. He learned to appreciate how disadvantaged people had turned to Marxism during the Great Depression in the West as a ray of hope in a dismal world. He was unable later to agree with many skeptics in the West who used to say that Marxists were frauds, that they were not believers, but careerists who masked their careerism in high sounding phrases. He concluded that for some Marxists the current runs deep. To be sure, some of those who spouted Marxism were frauds. They were saying what had to be said at the time to survive; however, for the majority—both among the foreign group and among the Soviet law students themselves—there was commitment. It was commonplace to hear students say: "My father cleaned toilets while I am to be a jurist." When one student was assigned, at the end of the course, to become dean of one of the new two year law schools in which the difficulties of organization with inadequate staff were apparent to all, he said to Hazard when queried on what he would expect: "Of course it will be hard. Of course I may fail and be punished for failure, but it is my duty as a Party member to do as I am told." With this spirit Tovarishch Dudnik set out for Kazan.

Graduation assignments were not always accepted with such grace. Under the rules, those who received stipends for the four year course were required to serve two years at a place assigned to them by a committee of the Ministry of Justice. Each student in turn left the classroom to go before the committee for assignment. Each had filed a statement telling where he or she would like to work and why. Some expressed the desire not to be separated from a spouse or gave some health reason. Most returned to the room to tell the others during the recess where they must go. Most were assigned to the far reaches of the country: Central Asia, Siberia, the Far North. When one woman returned, she started complaining aloud about her lot. The Party organizer for the group began humming the Internationale. Grumbling stopped.

Another woman used her head. She did not ask for Moscow or Leningrad or Kiev or Odessa, as others had done. She told Hazard later that she had asked for the provinces, as she knew that is where she would have to go. She had considered the places way out there in the provinces, and had decided that the most attractive was the Black Sea resort of Yalta. She asked for it and was placed there. She proved how one survives under an allocation system. Difficult as the allocation system was, students seemed to favor it over what they heard was the system in the West. They said they could not have faced the system in the United States where a graduate of a law school has to find a job for himself or herself. They preferred the assignment system to that.

Evening lectures brought prominent Soviet lawyers to the podium of the Institute: Vyshinsky, Pashukanis, and Krylenko. Vyshinsky received world-wide notoriety as the prosecutor at the Purge Trials of the 1930's. He prosecuted Bukharin, Radek, Krestinsky, and the other colleagues of Stalin of the early years who had lost favor by the mid-1930's. The second was the head of the Institute of State and Law of the U.S.S.R. Academy of Sciences, and as such was in charge of directing legal thought in the U.S.S.R. He also had the practical task of preparing the draft of the 1936 constitution. Krylenko was the man who had headed the codification effort of the N.E.P. period for the Commissariat of Justice, and was later to become the Commissar himself.

Vyshinsky lectured on court procedure in France. He had been a Menshevik before the revolution and came from a prominent family who had lived near the Polish frontier in the Empire. He stood on shaky political ground, in spite of having switched to Bolshevism, and ultimately to Stalin's faction. Hazard saw him as a man trying to save his own neck, an abject servant of his boss. Undoubtedly, he was a cultured man with remarkably broad knowledge of Western law. He lectured well, throwing expressions in several languages. One stood out in English when he said in heavily accented words, "De proof of de pooding is in de eating." His *leit motif* was that French procedure was designed to handicap the accused.

Pashukanis was a different type. He had been a judge in the first courts set up after the revolution. As a Latvian he was in a minority, but he was clever. He came to the fore as a scholar in the early 1920's when he developed the theory that law had its origin in the market place; that it was based upon exchange. The codes, in consequence, read like a menu in that each crime had a price that was exacted when the act was committed. He thought that civil law was the law of private exchange in the market, and that as socialism was advanced, there would be no reason for it still to be applied. It would wither away, as Marx and Engels had predicted it would under communism; it would do so by degrees as state enterprise replaced the N.E.P.'s private enterprise. In consequence, he ordered his lieutenants, among whom stood Amfiteatrov, to teach that civil law would be replaced by "economic law." He went further; he and his colleagues drafted codes to replace the N.E.P. codes, and many thought that by 1930 these drafts would become law.

Pashukanis was a tyrant among the law professors. They feared him, and even Korovin had to eat crow when Pashukanis attacked his theory of the international law of the transitional period. Pashukanis argued that all law was bourgeois and would remain so. Its future was to wither away, not to be transformed into a new Soviet law. In February 1937 he was purged. The law students heard about it when they returned from the January recess. Hazard was sitting in his class in criminal law, when the professor droned along in his lecture with his nose in his notes and said unexpectedly, "That enemy of the people, Pashukanis." Hazard looked at the man next to him. Had they heard correctly? "Enemy of the people" was the worst possible charge. It usually meant execution. When they left for vacation, Pashukanis was "king" of the law fraternity. Now he was an "enemy of the people." Soon his closest associates in the law institute were removed from their chairs. The books that had been used to teach economic law were withdrawn and replaced with new ones entitled "Civil and Economic Law."

The change in theory was so marked that Hazard was asked to return to Moscow in the fall of 1937 to repeat the course on theory of state and law. The Dean suggested that if he left, as had been planned, without knowledge of the change, he would be functioning with a discarded theoretical base for Soviet law. Of course, the suggestion was accepted, and the course was repeated under Professor Stalgevich who had the unenviable task of repudiating the old and improvising in the new. One morning, as the class filed out, one of the boys of peasant stock leaned down close to Hazard's ear and whispered, "Don't believe all you hear."

Krylenko shared with Pashukanis in organizing the draft of new codes to replace the N.E.P. codes. He was bracketed with Pashukanis in the purge, and he also was removed from his role as People's Commissar of Justice. He had never seemed to Hazard to be an intellectual heavyweight although he wrote some of the hardest-to-understand prose among the legal writers. It was old-fashioned literary prose with word orders very much out of the Western order and even of the current Soviet favored word order. It was similar to Latin, since the declensions had to be watched with great care to see which was subject, object, and their adjectival modifiers.

Krylenko's task as Commissar was to come annually to the Law Institute to hear student complaints. When he arrived, all students, professors, charwomen, and kitchen girls went to the auditorium. The charwomen sat in the front row with red bandanas over their hair. They reminded Hazard of the stories of Mme. Lafarge during the French Revolution. They were evident proof that there had been a revolution. Krylenko was attacked by the students because of poor food, messy rooms, and a bad program. He paced back and forth upon the stage, his shaved head shining in the bright lights, the epitome of the hard-boiled revolutionary. He admitted that all had not come up to his expectations, but things would improve.

Not all was work at the Institute. On free days, there was often a dance in the evening arranged by the trade union. A small brass orchestra was hired for the occasion. The trade union organizer, a woman student, would admonish the boys to wear collars and keep sober. Many came in their native costumes from the parts of the U.S.S.R. where modernization had not proceeded far. It was colorful. On other occasions the dances were to phonograph records at a student's flat. Hazard used to bring some of these records back from his summer trips abroad. He also brought paper patterns from Macy's and sat in the kitchen of one of the women to translate "top," "bottom," etc., so that they would know how to put the patterns together to cut out a dress in what was presumed to be the latest American mode.

On some weekends there were trips to the country on the commuting train to ski. The snows were deep; the pine trees drooped under the weight. The country looked like a Christmas card. At midday, there would be a stop at the rest house available to those within the system of the People's Commissariat of Justice. All sat at long tables, and students might be next to a judge or a janitor. After lunch was the "dead hour," when all had to recline in canvas chairs to rest for a time under the supervision of a nurse dressed in a baggy white sack pulled over her warm clothes.

Exam followed exam, and the course was drawing to a close for Hazard and his classmates. They had come to know each other well, at least for those who were not the Communist Party secretaries of the class. The latter never had anything to do with Hazard. His friends were among the nonparty students, or those who had no special role within the Party. The most sympathetic to him were the Jews and the mountain people from the Caucasus. The Jews had relatives in the West, and they liked contacts with the West. The mountain peoples were probably just curious to meet a Western type. Hazard always took the precaution of telling these friends nothing that they could not repeat, under torture if that occurred, about what he was saying. He knew what Stalin's tactics were, and he did not want to subject his friends to that sort of punishment for having known a foreigner.

It was true that he continued to see the American Embassy officers while he was in Moscow. His first Ambassador, William C. Bullitt, had told him at the first interview that he would, of course, be watched and that under the circumstances, it would be wise to report on his trips to the Embassy to collect his mail, to a Mr. Bender, who directed the auto pool. Bullitt said he was the chief police informer. Hazard never failed to tell Bender what he was doing, and, indeed, to conduct himself so that there was no reason not to tell all.

Later when Joseph Davies arrived, since he was a prominent lawyer, Hazard struck up a friendship with him. His daughter, Emlen, went with Hazard to the lectures at the Law Institute for a while, and Hazard was invited to Embassy parties and to lunch. He told Davies what was being done when Pashukanis was ousted. Later on, when Davies wrote his memoirs, he told of a conversation at one such luncheon. The Soviet security people may well have thought this paragraph in the memoirs proof that Hazard had always been a spy within their loose definition.

Embassy afternoons under Bullitt were given to the showing of American movies. Radek, Borodin, and Bukharin attended. At one dance the noted Marshall Tukhachevsky and his wife attended, looking for all the world like a cultured couple from the West. Hazard came to meet them all, and when they were all executed during the purges, he caught himself thinking that it would be good if the Germans did invade and kill the Stalin crowd. He doubted that any of these people had been traitors to the cause of 1917.

The last day came at the Law Institute at the end of the fall term 1937. Hazard was standing at the street car stop in front of the Institute, and one of his mountain friends was talking and saying good-bye. "Ivan Ivanovich," he said, "When you arrived, we did not expect you to declare yourself for us. We knew that you had no knowledge of what we were doing. Now, you have been with us for three years. If you are not with us after all you have learned, you must be an enemy." Thus ended, with the clarity and directness of the new generation, the three years. There is a barricade, and for the communists of that time, at least, one is on either one side or the other. There can be no in-between.

Chapter Three
WALL STREET

WALL STREET

Right after lunch the telephone rang in the office at Columbia University where Hazard was completing a month as a visiting lecturer in 1939. It was a law school classmate who had lived across the courtyard in 1934. "Would you like to have an interview for a job? I have just had lunch with a managing partner of a prominent law firm who needs a man your age. I have suggested you."

It was a bolt from heaven as far as Hazard was concerned. He was all prepared as a specialist on Soviet law, but nobody in 1939 wanted to hear about it. The Soviet leaders were becoming increasingly unpopular, and although the Hitler-Stalin pact had not yet even been imagined in the West, the smell of war in the air was slowing down commercial activity. A chance to enter a law firm as an associate, even simply to practice New York law like the others who had not taken years off to study other topics, seemed all that Hazard could hope for. He was quick to reply, "I shall call up immediately and arrange an appointment."

In this surprising way, there began a two-year association with colleagues at the New York Bar which was to last until the Germans invaded the U.S.S.R. in 1941. The interview went well. The applicant asked only that he be given until July to report so that he might return to the U.S.S.R. for one last visit. He now had his doctorate from the University of Chicago, and he had been admitted to the Bar in 1935, so the preliminaries had been completed. It was now time to settle down to work, even though it was not the kind of practice he and the Institute of Current World Affairs had hoped for.

That brief interlude before practice was a sobering one. The smell of war was stronger when he reached Moscow in late May. By the time he had completed his visit and reached Kiev in preparation for leaving the U.S.S.R. war seemed in the offing. He took the little train leading to the Ukrainian-Polish frontier. As it proceeded, more and more people left the cars until, at the frontier station, he and one other man were the last two passengers in the car that had to be pushed across into Poland. He naturally spoke to his fellow passenger and learned that he was the Polish Consul-General in Kiev returning home to file a report. The time was June 1939.

After reaching the Polish side of the frontier and clearing the border controls, the train began to pick up passengers. Many were officers in uniform and also dead drunk. The Consul-General, who was sitting in a first class coupé in the car, came into Hazard's second class coupé to invite him into the first class space. He indicated that it was mobilization day for the officers of the Polish army in anticipation of war, and the officers would be drunk after farewell parties. They might be annoying or even dangerous. Hazard readily accepted the invitation, and they rolled on to Lvov together. The train became standing room only with the officers who got on at every stop.

Hazard's former roommate, with whom he studied international law in Geneva in the summer of 1932, was waiting to receive him. He was, at this point, a judge in the Polish court at Lvov, explaining that his task was to sentence quite a few communists for crime. Hazard told him that Soviet law had become his specialty and asked if his friend knew any Soviet law. He replied, "I suppose I ought to learn some since we are so near the border, but I have never taken the time." Within a few weeks he was a prisoner of the Soviet Army as it rolled into Lvov under the terms of the Hitler-Stalin pact. Later, he died in a Kiev prison of pneumonia, or so the story went from those who had escaped from the Soviet Army through Romania as it rolled in.

Hazard continued on through the Balkans, sensing that the war would go through this area. He stopped in Romania and visited Kishinev. Kishinev was the capital of the Russian Imperial province of Bessarabia which had passed to Romania after World War I. At that town he sought a hotel room, speaking first in English, then in French and finally, having no success, in Russian. The proprietor pointed to a sign in Romanian which was on the wall behind him. Hazard could not read it and said so in Russian. The proprietor was then all smiles and responded in perfect Russian that it said: only Romanian may be spoken here. But, if a guest did not know it, another language might be used. Signs of hatred of the Russians by the Romanian government were everywhere. Even the easily identifiable statue of Pushkin in the city park had a space below it in the plinth from which the marble had been chipped away to remove identification, presumably in the Cyrillic alphabet. Although this had long been a city of Russian names, all street signs were in Romanian.

The trip went on through Bulgaria and Yugoslavia. Then the Orient Express from Belgrade took Hazard to Milan where an old family friend waited on the platform to greet him. She said she feared that the war would begin any minute, and hoped that he would be able to cross the line into Switzerland, that night, before it began. Hazard thought of his father and Grandmother in 1914 when they were caught in Germany at the outbreak of the war. He wondered whether history was to be repeated. With such fears, it was with relief that he heard the Swiss passport officer in the corridor at the frontier and knew that he was safely in the "West."

Law practice began quietly. It was as if the war clouds were not yet in sight. Baldwin, Todd & Young, although an old respected firm, included only fourteen partners and as many associates. The firm's managing partner, who had interviewed Hazard, was a Williams graduate of the old school philosophy—a perfect gentleman. When Hazard asked about the firm's work-hours, the partner told him that unlike law sweatshops this firm believed associates should work decent hours so they would have time available when real crises occurred. It was agreed that the associates could go home for dinner, although some of the young lawyers stayed on to eat dinner at the client's expense and then returned to work until 11 p.m. Hazard found it preferable to take the subway early, before the crowds arrived at 8 a.m., so he could give a long day's service and work until 6:30 p.m. Perhaps the years of early rising as a child to practice the violin, made it easier for Hazard to adapt to such a schedule.

Being a small firm, it was splendid for an apprenticeship. Unlike some of the large firms where there had developed a division of labor, this firm did not assign an associate to a single type of work to continue for years. It gave young lawyers a chance to do much of everything. Associates were assigned to a partner who had priority claims upon their time, but any partner could ask for service. The associate had to become a diplomat and keep everyone happy. He could not say: "I am busy with Mr. Rose's work." Milton C. Rose was, indeed, Hazard's mentor, and a good one he was, too. Also a Williams man, he had the courteous manners associated, at the time, with such graduates. He always was considerate, but he wanted work done right. He would send back a draft again and again until it was the way he wanted. He made his secretary retype documents which supposedly had been in their final form. He allowed no erasures. As the years went on, he proved the merit of his approach and rose to become the senior partner in one of the largest Wall Street firms with which his smaller firm had merged.

July and August 1939 passed quietly by as Hazard learned the ropes. Fortunately, a fellow classmate from the Harvard Law School was also an associate, and he gave Hazard practical advice. Hazard was solely what the British would call a solicitor. He never went to court except to answer a calendar during the summer vacation of one of the litigators. At the time, no firm wanted litigation since it was said to cost more than the fees that could be charged. Most law work was that of the solicitor variety. Rose's specific clients were the members of the late Willard Straight's family. They had a wide variety of interests. The most exciting to Hazard was the fact that as principal owners of the *New Republic* they took an active part in its affairs. Rose took Hazard to the monthly board meetings, and it was at these meetings that he came to know the editor,

Bruce Bliven, well. Bliven remained Hazard's friend throughout his life until his death in his advanced eighties.

New Republic board meetings had little law in them. They were primarily devoted to editorial policy and to gossip about the state of the nation. Had this association come when Hazard was still in law school, he might have thought the editors far to the left. However, with the experience Hazard gained in Russia, he could easily distinguish a communist from a liberal. Bliven and his colleagues certainly did not want revolution. They wanted to patch up the American system so that it would be more humanistic. They were Roosevelt liberals with an eye on the welfare of the common man but not government by those unprepared for it. Roosevelt was their hero, and he was no common man.

On September 1, 1939, the war broke out. Hazard was at home with the young lawyers with whom he lived. At that time, few young men thought of marrying before they got their feet on the ground, and they joined in groups of four to rent apartments which they ran communally. Indeed, they had to combine their earnings since the starting salary for a law associate was $2,800 a year, with a raise of $500 at the first Christmas after beginning work. On an individual basis, this was not very much money, but since they were living at prices of the Great Depression it was adequate, for they combined their salaries and were able, as a result, to pay the rent, buy food, and even hire a cook-valet who took care of them with a certain aplomb.

Into that environment, on September 1, Hitler marched into Poland. Hazard sat at the radio and listened to King George VI of England make the historic announcement that England would come to the aid of its ally. Hazard remembered Lord Grey's famous statement when the First World War began that: "The lights of Europe are going out." Having just returned from Europe, Hazard had a lump in his throat as he listened to that impeccably proper English voice describe the beginning of horrors the likes of which no one could comprehend nor know how long they would last. Those with knowledge of history expected the United States to be brought into the conflict, but there was no evidence of this in practice.

Days were taken up with the usual inconsequential and unromantic details of a general practice. There were wills to be drafted and witnessed. There were corporations to be formed, the more so because one client had owned many guaranteed mortgages, and when the guarantor went bankrupt during the depression, the client had taken over the mortgages, himself. This meant that each property had to be managed, and to do so without fear that a losing one would drag down all the rest, each property was set up as a separate corporation. The numbers were large, and every day there were two or three incorporations to be conducted in accordance with a model established some time earlier when the first certificate had to be converted into the new form.

Lawyers had to become clerks to the good clients. Even if they wanted to hire a cook, a lawyer was called upon to make the arrangements. When a friend needed a U.S. entry visa, a lawyer had to go to Ellis Island to arrange it. The only advantage of such a menial chore was the fact that it permitted Hazard to put on his time sheet some hours which were without pressure as he waited at the ferry slip for the ferry to arrive. Out of one such case, he made a friend who helped him keep up his Russian. She was an elderly Russian gentlewoman without funds but in need of help at the Immigration Service. In return for the service, it was agreed by his firm, she would meet with Hazard weekly and listen to him read Russian. This started what proved to be a great help, for Russian, like any language, slips away if unused. With this weekly hour of reading and marking texts with the proper accent and gossiping before and after about anything and everything, he kept his Russian language alive. This made it possible for him, when he went to Washington in 1941 to join the Lend-Lease staff, to step immediately into his liaison work with the Soviet officials with whom he had to deal.

Perhaps the lasting impact of practice was from its emphasis upon fruitful use of time. Every lawyer kept a diary on which he or she recorded what was done every fifteen minutes throughout the day. Some client or the firm itself must be charged, and the accountant posted the items on the client's account each night so that bills could be prepared at any time to cover the work completed. Hazard learned, as did all other lawyers, to listen to the metronome ticking in his ears at all times. He was trained not to waste a minute of expensive time. In a sense he became an automaton, for he worked without thinking about how unpleasant it might have seemed under difficult circumstances to keep track of the minutes. The ground was laid to turn him into a workaholic. For long years subsequently, when there were no clients to be charged; when as an academic he was given total freedom to choose when to work and when not to work, except for the obligation to meet classes at the assigned hours, he heard the metronome ticking away. It startled him to see others who had not had such experience use their time with no thought to its value. When those he met used to ask: "How do you get so much done in a day?" the answer was easy: "I worked in Wall Street."

Despite the fact that practice offered little of a romantic character, there were some moments of amusement. On one such memorable occasion, one of the partners said he had a Norwegian client who had lived in the South Seas and had hit upon the scheme of creating a new race of men and women who would be half Norwegian and half Polynesian. They would multiply and eventually take over from the Chinese the entrepreneurial positions in the pearl diving business, and thus, elevate the poor Polynesians, who had been limited up to that time to menial jobs of diving, to a more lucrative level. Hazard was asked to draw up a marriage contract, valid under the French law of the Tahitian archipelago, which would bind the parties to work together in such a relationship. Of course, such a binding contract would have been illegal in the U.S.A. and considered a form of "slavery," but no one quite knew whether it would be valid under the Civil Law of the area.

The whole idea sounded a bit odd, but an assignment was an assignment. The years have blurred what Hazard discovered as the law on the topic, but he remembers preparing a contract, and binding the pages together with blue ribbons and gold seals hoping to impress local magistrates with its seriousness. He was invited to attend the marriage ceremony at the City Clerk's office up the street. When he arrived and met the Polynesian bride, it was quickly evident she was pregnant. The Norwegian client had apparently not waited for the contract to be drafted. They were wed; signatures were affixed, and one can only hope that they lived happily ever after and started a new race of man.

The only matter involving Soviet law that came into the office in those two years on Wall Street was brought in by Hazard, himself. The firm encouraged associates to find their own business and gave them a percentage of the fee to add to their regular salary. In this case, friends in the community in New York who followed Soviet affairs came to Hazard to tell him they wanted to go into the business of importing music from the Soviet Union. They wanted to incorporate and to have his help in negotiating a contract with a Soviet music exporting firm which would assure them of a monopoly on the importation of music for first American performances.

The incorporation was, of course, easy because it had been learned as a routine with the mortgage certificate cases. The negotiations were more difficult, and Hazard got his first taste of what he learned later to be the frustrations of negotiating with the Russians. Again and again it would appear that agreement had been reached on contract terms only to learn, a few days later, that the Soviet side wanted to reopen the issue. On the question of price, there was endless haggling. It seemed at times that there would be no contract. Finally, the great day arrived when all was in order, and the Soviet agents from Amtorg Trading Corporation invited the Americans to a signing party, and a dinner at Longchamps restaurant in the Empire State Building, one of the exclusive places to eat at the time. Of course, the occasion was festive. The vodka flowed, although

Hazard never did more than sip it. He had learned during his student days in Moscow that it upsets the system more permanently than getting drunk for an evening. He developed the technique of telling his hosts that he was too young to drink. This caused them to laugh outright because he was already balding. They did not continue to press. This technique stood him in good stead during his subsequent work at Lend-Lease in Washington. Vodka was always offered to soften the resolution of the Americans so that they would not deny a Soviet request, and the Soviet hosts made it hard for their guests to say "no."

Regrettably, the contract was not always honored on the provisions for monopoly of first performances. Koussevitsky would be given the first performance at the Boston Symphony without any evident payment for the privilege, and the little New York music corporation would be left with the first commercial deal from which the glamor of an American premiere had been removed.

Looking back upon those Wall Street years, the memories that remained were of habits acquired: meticulous care in all that was done; avoidance of wasted time; conduct of several operations at the same time, giving them all attention and keeping them all in the air like the balls of a juggler; handling papers so that none was misplaced; and, of course, developing a manner with clients that kept them happy and inclined to return when they had their next problem. An apprenticeship in law practice, when conducted under the supervision of a skilled attorney, is good schooling for a man of affairs in government, in teaching, and in participating in professional associations when responsibilities are given by colleagues by election to office.

As a professor at Columbia University, this latter activity became a pleasurable sideline to his teaching career which he undertook upon his return to New York City after WWII. Activities focussed on associations of lawyers and associations of Slavicists. Hazard became Secretary of the American Association for the Advancement of Slavic Studies, which he helped create. He served on the Executive Council of the American Society of International Law and eventually became a Vice-President. He served on the Executive Committee of the American Foreign Law Association and eventually became its President. He served on the Executive Committee of the American Branch of the International Law Association and eventually became its President, and he served on the Executive Committee of the International Association of Legal Science and eventually became its President. In all of these activities, the experience of the Wall Street apprenticeship seemed to have best fitted him for the offices he was given. Fellow members evidently felt that with Hazard in the chair, things would get done.

Chapter Four
MARRIAGE AND FAMILY

MARRIAGE AND FAMILY

Girls were to be adored on a pedestal and not taken to bed until marriage. That was the Yankeeland ethic, and a great deal of it wore off in reality on the young lads of conservative families in the north. Of course, there were parties, dances, dinners and an occasional kiss during a game of "post office," but there was no dating with the meaning that word came to have in the 1960's. Every boy wanted to have several girls, and there was no thought of pairing off. The sexual revolution was still thirty years away.

Hazard was engulfed in these mores. Perhaps subconsciously his teenage sister, seven years older than he, was his model. Ruddy-cheeked, well-scrubbed, athletic, a good mixer but always holding boys at arms' length, she was one of the attractive girls of Syracuse. The young brother seems to have developed the same type of girl as his ideal. Indeed, some years later when he was driving his mother on a motor trip through Scotland shortly before her death in 1930, he remarked as a Yankee type passed by the window: "That is the type of girl I want to marry." History provided circumstances which made that dream come into being.

Of course, not all men of the era had such ideas. Everyone knew who went to Yale which group of fellows hit the prostitutes on Chapel Street. They were never scorned, but they were not brought into an inner circle of friends by the great majority. Perhaps the restraints of that era were not all Platonic. Yale doctors took the precaution of showing freshmen, soon after arrival, films of men wobbling along sidewalks struggling under the limitations of V.D. The danger of intercourse was played up. For the women, the perils of pregnancy were made known. This was not to say that there were no trysts for loving. They were, however, very secret. If a girl from a so-called good family had the misfortune to become pregnant, the situation was not hopeless. Safe havens existed in the woods where she could appear to retire — as if on vacation — have her baby, have it put up for adoption and then forgotten. The pill had not even been dreamed of at the time. Abstinence was, therefore, a necessity if couples wanted to keep out of trouble, but that trouble was by no means the only motive to keep to what was generally preached and accepted as the better way to spend the years before marriage. The mores of the day were an important factor.

Hazard followed the rules, and his friends did too. One was not surrounded by temptation either, because coeducation in preparatory school at Yale or at the Harvard Law School did not exist. There were proms at Vassar and weekends at Smith. These were "proper" affairs, but that did not mean they were boring events. In Law School, there were only two married men in the class, and at Yale there were none. Men waited for post-graduation to choose a partner. In Hazard's case, the period of waiting was lengthened by the terms of his fellowship to study in Moscow. The Director of the Foundation who sent him cautioned that if he were to marry, his fellowship would end. This was not a puritanical rule but one based upon reason. He argued that experience had shown that a student in a foreign land became cut off from his fellows if he had a wife in the apartment who did not know the language, had nothing to do, and awaited his return in the evening to monopolize his time. From the Director's viewpoint, learning another strange culture required that the student be free to join the students of the host country in their play as well as their work. A wife at home is simply an impediment.

With these restraints Hazard gave no thought to choosing a mate once his fellowship began. Before that time, he had, of course, his favorite girls. At his twenty-first birthday party in Syracuse, he had his table set with a gorgeous brunette on one side and a gorgeous blonde on the other. Both were favorite candidates, but for a rather distant future. In prepschool he wrote almost daily to a southern belle he had met in Virginia while visiting his school roommate. She was invited to the Senior prom, and even to a weekend or so at Yale. But once Russia came into the picture, there was no further thought given to making choices. To avoid temptation, he put any close friendships with the female Soviet classmates out of his mind. They were just like the boys: good friends with whom dances and ski trips, but nothing more, were arranged. He kept himself free to associate with everyone and learned all he could of the culture.

Only upon his return to New York to begin the practice of law was the situation changed. Living with three other men in a communal apartment made it possible to meet people. Each of them would bring home to dinner interesting characters and attractive women. But, none seemed to meet the description formulated in Scotland in 1929. Finally, the day came, quite unexpectedly, of course. The occasion was the marriage of one of the men with whom the trip around the world had been taken in 1930-31. It was to be held on a Friday afternoon in June 1940 at the home of the bride on Long Island. She was one of several sisters who were well known and much admired by the young men in Hazard's circle. He had known her for many years. The problem for Hazard was how to get permission to attend the wedding.

With some fear, he approached the managing partner of the law firm where he worked. The man's response was: "You will never become a successful lawyer if you run off on Friday afternoons." In spite of this warning, the consent was given, and off he went on that fateful day.

After the ceremony in the bride's living room, the wedding party and guests retired to the rose garden. All of a sudden, there she was walking among the roses in a perky white saucer hat tilted on her bobbed hair, a ruddy complexion, no make-up, a healthy look, and turned-up nose. She resembled the "Gibson girl" made famous in so many sketches by its famous creator. Hazard approached cautiously because it simply was not acceptable to be brash in those days. He started a conversation and learned that she was a cousin of the bride; lived in Springfield, Massachusetts; was a nursery school teacher, and had studied for her profession at a New York school. Hazard's mind was made up right then and there, but how could he meet her again? To his delight and relief, he learned that she would be coming to New York the following winter to complete her last year of college and receive her degree. Nothing more was said. They moved toward her car to meet her mother and waved good-bye as she drove down the road to return to Springfield.

Now, began the planning stage. How could a meeting be arranged with the Springfield belle that would not be too obvious yet meet the requirements of the mores of the time? Fortunately, one of Hazard's former roommates had a charming mother with whom Hazard discussed his problem. She suggested a general welcome party for new arrivals in New York to be held at her home in the fall. It would be an occasion for local boys to meet visiting belles, and, of course, the Springfield belle would be included as just a member of the group.

Hazard's roommates were, of course, privy to the plans, and the great day came with all of them present. The young lady finally arrived, moved to the fireplace and stood in front of the mantle while engaged in casual conversation, stepped over to a corner chair, where the conversation continued until it was time to go home. At that point, one of Hazard's roommates came over to say casually, "John, we are going home. Do you want to join us?" It was like a signal. Hazard leaned forward and asked the young lady if he could take her home in a taxi. She, fortunately and perhaps inevitably, said yes, so, off they went. Arrangements were made to meet for supper at an Austrian restaurant near her apartment, and invitations to the table of the four roommates followed so frequently that it became obvious that the courting was proceeding at great speed. Still, caution was required. The young lady's roommate sent word to Hazard, that he must not hurry things, or he would not succeed.

The winter moved ahead, and Hazard caught the flu so seriously that he was put to bed for several days. His new friend came to visit, and he could not continue with the "friendship" relationship. He penned a letter setting forth his thoughts; got no direct reply, but did receive an invitation to visit the family home in Springfield for a weekend. Of course, he accepted and took the train on the appointed day to be greeted by a huge family which consisted of the father, the mother and seven children, one of whom had recently been married. The father was an Episcopalian Bishop. Hazard had been reared an Episcopalian by his southern mother, although his father, a Rhode Islander, had been a Congregationalist. Episcopalianism was, therefore, Hazard's background, and the Bishop did not frighten him, the more so since he was a very informal, kindly man. The Mother seemed, at first glance, to be a "proper Bostonian" with a heart of gold and the mark of simplicity characteristic of that type of woman.

In the big living room before the fireplace, and from a seat across the room, Hazard asked the young lady if he would be acceptable. The answer was affirmative so he moved closer. But, just at that moment, the bride of the married brother came down the stairs and bounced in to enliven the conversation. She guessed that something was afoot but waited a moment to talk so as not to be too obvious, and then retired. That evening, Susan Lawrence told her parents that Hazard had proposed, and they seemed pleased. The die was cast, leaving only the date to be set. It was February, and Lent was at hand. No one could marry properly during Lent, and engagements were expected to be long. Those were the rules of a Boston family, but the draft was creeping up on Hazard. Neither thought it wise to wait too long.

In spite of misgivings from the Lawrences, and especially from Susan's mother, a date early in March 1941 was set. Arrangements were completed for a service at the Cathedral, and a reception at the home was planned. Hazard brought his sister, his mother's former companion, and friends to Springfield. His brother was too far away to attend. A family supper, with the bride-to-be, was held at the local hotel and afterwards the snow began to fall. It fell all night, and by morning there was a question as to whether anyone could reach the Cathedral, and whether the guests from out of town could reach Springfield. The bride's grandfather, the retired Bishop of Massachusetts, had to cancel his planned attendance, but a great many of the other guests reached Springfield. The very heavy snows added to the festiveness and informality of the occasion. Robert Bowie, a Harvard Law classmate with whom Hazard spent several summers on canoe and pack trips, was best man. Susan's three sisters were bridesmaids. All went well despite the snow. The couple left after the reception and went by train to New York City, where they borrowed an apartment for a honeymoon and an abode in which to start their home while looking for something more permanent.

On June 22, 1941 the war began for the Soviets. Hazard was soon called to Washington. His bride was not yet finished with her final term leading to her B.S. in Education, so she could only come down to Washington for weekends to Hazard's hotel. Finally, when the degree was safely in her portfolio, she joined Hazard in Washington. They rented an apartment and settled down.

From the family point of view, Washington was the time for children. Three were born in Washington while the fourth was born after the war when the couple returned to New York and Hazard was teaching at Columbia. Those were busy days for Hazard, as his work at the office went from seven to seven. On the weekends, he tried to write articles for the law reviews, but there was no free time. The family inevitably suffered, but Susan kept it alive in good fashion. She was an old-fashioned girl who did not sense the need for a career outside the family to prove herself. For her, the family, itself, was an honorable career to which she gave herself wholeheartedly.

The arrival of the first child was symbolic of the times. Susan reported in the middle of the first practice blackout that the baby was on the way. The couple arose and used a flashlight to find their way to the door of the apartment house. A cab was found with its headlights shielded by a black orb in which a small cross was cut to show where the car was. Off they went to the Garfield hospital. Some days later, Hazard received a letter from the warden on their block saying that a flashlight had been seen in his apartment during the blackout, and that this was an offense. He responded with a letter that explained the unusual circumstances and heard nothing more. Evidently the warden had a heart.

Pressure at the office was so great that Hazard had to go off to work that morning without word as to whether the baby had arrived. He was already hard at work, dictating to his early morning secretary, when his phone rang. Dr. Brown announced that a boy had arrived and all was well, but his wife was still under ether, and there was no point for him to come to the hospital until later in the day. Thus, John Gibson, named for Hazard's father, came into a turbulent world filled with blackouts and fears.

William and Nancy were to follow, and both were healthy babies. Those were the days when mothers remained at the hospital for many days and returned home to stay in bed again for many days with a nurse in attendance. But all went well, and there were no complications. The apartment where John was born proved too small with its single bedroom. He cried frequently and for long periods of time. Doctors were not yet in favor of demand feeding. Parents waited for appointed feeding times and suffered the wails that followed. Hazard could not stand it. He moved into the living room and could not wait for mornings. At work, he was so tired he could not wait to go home. A cartoon of James Thurber caught his eye. It showed one of Thurber's famous shapeless characters slumped in a huge stuffed chair. The caption read: "I have never been the same since the birth of my first child." Clearly, some new home was required, and Susan found it on a hillside. It was like Wendy's house in Peter Pan. The family moved in, and it was bliss for the rest of the Washington years.

Chapter Five
THE LEND-LEASE EPISODE

THE LEND-LEASE EPISODE

June 22, 1941 was a fateful day. Very early in the morning the Panzer Divisions of Hitler's Army, supported by the Romanians, began their drive into the East along a front that stretched from the Baltic to the Black Sea. The unprepared troops of Stalin's army were seemingly taken by surprise, for their commander-in-chief had refused to believe British and United States intelligence that the attack was in preparation. The historic pact of 1939 signed by Ribbentrop and Molotov under which Soviet troops had marched into Poland and the Baltic countries was thought to assure safety, but now the Hitler goals were clear. *Lebensraum* was to be wrested from Stalin, and unwillingly he was drawn into the war.

Churchill and Roosevelt saw their opportunity immediately. In spite of a career of Bolshevik-bating, Churchill called immediately for the reversal of policy and support of the Soviet armies. Although the United States was not yet at war with the Germans, Roosevelt was ready, also, to change from the hostility of the Hitler-Stalin pact years to one of aiding the Soviet Army. The embargo on all trade with the Soviets was lifted, and the Soviet Ambassador, Constantin Oumansky, was welcomed at the State Department with a list of material that Stalin wanted to buy. Roosevelt placed Sumner Welles in charge of the diplomatic moves, but he turned to his close friend, Harry Hopkins, to start the supplies flowing. Within the organization created to administer Lend-Lease to the British and bearing the euphemistic title Division of Defense Aid Reports, a new Soviet bureau was established under the direction of Colonel Philip R. Faymonville. The Colonel had served the first term after recognition of the U.S.S.R. as military attaché in the Moscow Embassy, and he had come to know the American student community, including Hazard.

Within days, the telephone rang in Hazard's Wall Street law office where he had been marking time for two years while no one wanted to trade with the Russians. Fortunately, he could fall back on his profession as a member of the New York Bar to which he had been admitted on completion of the Harvard Law School while still studying in Moscow. For two relatively uneventful years, he had engaged in the nitty-gritty of an ordinary law practice as an associate of a prominent but small firm, and had expected little opportunity to use what he had learned among the Russians. That phone call was to change everything.

It was Colonel Faymonville on the wire. "Could you come right down to Washington and discuss the possibility of joining the government to help liaison on supply matters with the Russians?" In a sense it

49

was a miracle that Hazard was still at his desk, for in April of that fateful year, he was the first in his office to be called to the draft. He won the pool that the young lawyers had created to give to the first to be called. He had even bid his bride of a month good-bye and trudged off to the medical examiner's office. To his surprise, he could not meet the then-rigorous eye test, and within an hour he was on his way back to his apartment to tell his wife the news. The next morning, he was back at his desk downtown to tell his comrades that the farewell party they had held for him had been premature. Consequently, he was back at work when Faymonville called.

Washington was in turmoil. Although the United States was not to be at war for another five months, people poured into the city to meet the build-up of personnel required to staff the supply offices which Roosevelt was creating. Within a day, Hazard had made his decision to join the government; had filled out the lengthy forms telling of his curious career among the Russians, and returned to New York to ask for leave at the law office to join the Civil Service. Clearance would take time, but the need for a staff on the Soviet desk in the supply program was so pressing that he was put to work immediately while clearance proceeded.

Oumansky was the principal point of liaison. He was not a pleasant man; indeed he gave the impression of a slippery operator of the Eastern European school. His primary contact was, of course, Harry Hopkins, but the details came to Faymonville and then to Hazard who was only the second man to be hired in the office. The Soviet list of requests was not long, but it came to a bureaucracy which was still mindful of the long years of non-recognition and the more recent hostile years of the Hitler-Stalin Pact. It was not to be moved quickly. Roosevelt knew this, and he gave Hopkins a short letter typed on green White House letterhead and signed by him with C. in C. under his name in the same handwriting. It called upon government officials to facilitate the supply of the items listed. It was Faymonville's and Hazard's task to clear the list through the reluctant bureaucracy of the State Department and the Army and Navy Munitions Board. Faymonville took on the Army to which he had devoted his life. The youthful Hazard, still only thirty-two years of age, was sent to State. His contact was the Assistant Secretary, Adolph Berle.

Berle was a wiry nervous man whose nose twitched as he spoke. He took the photostat of the historic C. in C. letter and turned to Hazard: "Don't you know young man that there are times when the President needs to be protected against himself?" With those words he stunned the messenger who thought the Commander-in-Chief's words were law. He could do nothing but repeat his orders and hope for the best, but he had learned his first lesson. Bureaucrats can nullify a President's policy. This was to begin his study of a great bureaucracy which was to lead to a professorship of public law at Columbia University when he returned to civilian life where he taught an introductory course that compared the American and Soviet bureaucracies.

By degrees the bureaucrats softened up, largely through pressures brought by Hopkins from the White House bedroom where he lived and worked.

The Soviet office in the Division of Defense Aid Reports grew modestly. Faymonville pushed hard and believed passionately that the only way to bring Hitler to task was to keep the Russians in the war. His colleagues in military intelligence were telling General George C. Marshall that the Soviet Army could not last, but Faymonville was sure it would. Hazard supported Faymonville's conclusions that the Komsomols, from whom the Army was drawn, had incredibly high morale which Hazard had sensed when he was a student. If morale could be considered a factor, there would be no surrender.

Of course, those who thought otherwise tried to poison the atmosphere by calling Faymonville a red, and some of the color washed off on his young assistant who supported him. But Hopkins was firm in his resolution, and his Chief of the Division of Defense Aid Supports, Major General James H. Burns, had enough influence in an Army where he had been Chief of Ordinance, to enforce discipline among its bureaucrats. It was an uphill fight, but the supplies began to trickle through as the Soviet Ambassador made himself increasingly unpopular with his almost panicky ways of hurrying from office to office. He urged, even threatened, to complain to Roosevelt personally. He tried to win friends by offering favors. He even hinted to Hazard that if all went well he could count on an honorary degree from the University of Moscow. Hazard knew enough about American views of those who received Soviet favors to imagine what that would do to his career. The hint was not repeated.

The summer and fall dragged on as Nazi troops marched toward Moscow. Hopkins flew with Averell Harriman to Moscow via the dangerous northern route around Norway. They saw Stalin; asked the routine questions on the state of Soviet supplies but received no answers. In desperation, they sent a cable to the White House informing the President that Stalin was mum. If the United States thought it necessary to defeat Hitler to keep Stalin in the war, the requirements of information would have to be waived. Roosevelt made his historic decision, and the supplies were released.

But, Soviet funds were running out. They could not continue to pay for all that they needed. Roosevelt decided to put the U.S.S.R. under Lend-Lease along with the British. November 7, 1941 was chosen as the day for action. It was, of course, the anniversary of the Russian Revolution. Roosevelt, with his flare for dramatic gesture, chose that day to make his announcement, but some preliminaries had to be complied with before the Lend-Lease Act could be applied. Under its terms, a recipient country would have to sign an agreement to pay royalties to owners of patents on items shipped under the program. This was where Hazard was brought in.

General Burns called Hazard into the front office about one o'clock in the afternoon and told him of Roosevelt's plan to announce inclusion of the U.S.S.R. under Lend-Lease during the Soviet Embassy reception in honor of their Revolution. That was to be about 5 P.M. The patent protocol had to be signed before that time, and Hazard was directed to get the signature. Oumansky had been recalled. No Ambassador had yet replaced him. The Soviet Chargé d'Affaires was Andrei Gromyko, who had been serving as counselor during Oumansky's term, and in that capacity Hazard had come to know him. Both men were thirty-two years old, but they differed greatly. Hazard had lived in the more-or-less protected society of the United States while Gromyko had learned to take the hard knocks of a communist bureaucracy and lived through Stalin's great purge of the late 1930's. He had survived while many of his colleagues in the diplomatic service, including Boris Skvirsky who had arranged Hazard's study in Moscow and Aleksei Neyman who had been Troyanovsky's counselor before Oumansky's term in Washington, were being purged and killed by Stalin. Gromyko was a careful man. Hazard knew this and told Burns that he could not imagine that Gromyko would sign the document without consulting with Moscow, therefore, the expected results could hardly be achieved by 5 P.M. Burns, good soldier that he was, told Hazard that he had to perform the President's command, and there was no alternative.

Gromyko agreed to see Burns' emissary, and off Hazard went to the Chancery of the Soviet Embassy on 16th Street. Gromyko's office was in the wing overlooking the little garden facing the street. When Hazard entered, he was seated at his desk. Hazard told him the purpose of the mission and presented the paper for signature fully expecting to hear that nothing could be done without Moscow's approval. To his surprise, Gromyko looked up after reading it thoroughly and said just this: "Have the British signed this?" Hearing that they had, Gromyko took the desk pen and signed his name across the bottom. To this day, it is not clear whether he had known the terms of the Act because he had done his homework, had obtained Moscow's consent well in advance and acted on that authority, or whether he took a most courageous step and committed his government to make payments in amounts no one could estimate. Whatever the reason, he signed, he acted, and the day was saved. The U.S.S.R. joined Britain as a major Lend-Lease recipient, and the reception went off as planned. An Office of the Lend-Lease Administration was soon created to replace the Division of Defense Aid Reports; Edward Stettinius was made the Administrator, and a U.S.S.R. Branch was created alongside branches for other recipients. Faymonville had been sent to Moscow to head the supply office in the Embassy and had been replaced in Washington by his good friend and West Point classmate: Brigadier General Sydney P. Spalding. Hazard remain in the number two position in the office, which grew swiftly to handle the increased volume of requests.

Although Stettinius was now nominally in charge of the Lend-Lease program for the U.S.S.R., Harry Hopkins was the court of last resort. A "Protocol" was agreed upon by the White House under Hopkins' direction, and it set forth in detail the quantities of supplies that would be delivered over the next year. From the worm's eye position of the staff of the U.S.S.R. branch of the Lend-Lease administration, Hopkins looked very high indeed. Every time a delay occurred—and some were inevitable—complaints would go to Hopkins from the Soviet Embassy. Hopkins was given an office in the White House in the Lincoln bedroom. A card table was set up for him at the foot of the bed and this served as his desk. He lived and worked in this room and held meetings and conferences with knowledgeable members of the Lend-Lease staff. On one memorable occasion he told Hazard: "I shall have to drag my old carcass over to see Patterson to get those trucks moving." And off he went with his staff support. He was evidently a very sick man, but with indomitable courage which inspired the youngsters of the staff.

Stettinius was a product of big business. He had become used to delegating authority and to have his own personal staff to brief him. Bob Lynch and Hayden Raynor digested every report and told him orally each morning what he needed to know. Since they were overwhelmed with documents, it was necessary to reduce all information to fit on a single page, and special large-type typewriters were used to prepare these pages. Of course, this made the information shorter.

The situation would have been intolerable for the staff who had much to say, had it not been for a very special assistant Stettinius had sitting in a room close by his office. This was the *eminence grise* of his administration, a man who had been a great friend of his father and a loving "uncle" to Stettinius himself. His assignment was to read anything he wanted, to talk with anyone he wanted, and to give Stettinius—from time to time—his wise assessment of the situation. Although the Soviets often called upon Stettinius, they never caught sight of John Pratt, his adviser, but the staff knew him as a friend. He would listen, draw conclusions and advise his protégé, whom he, of course, called Ed. Later, when Stettinius was moved to the Department of State as the Secretary, John Pratt was taken along to perform the same invaluable function. He never lost touch with the Soviet situation throughout the war. Indeed, in the Department he once called Hazard to his desk to report that Stalin's representative at the Dumbarton Oaks conference considering the structure of a United Nations had asked for a seat for every one of the Soviet Republics within the U.S.S.R. Pratt was trying to devise a strategy to counter the request. All the world now knows that the compromise was to give seats to the Ukraine and Bielorussia on the grounds that these two Republics had suffered most from the war. The others were given no voice directly in the membership.

Since the Lend-Lease program of supplies was coordinated closely with the British government so as to avoid overlapping requests or duplicate supplies, the American staff spent considerable time with the British office in Washington. Early in the relationship, Hazard found himself taken along to a conference. To his surprise, the opposite numbers were not Englishmen, but two Canadians and a Frenchman. The Frenchman was a dynamic, very small man who seemed intensely concerned with the plans. Hazard wondered why a Frenchman should appear at all. He was introduced as Jean Monnet, a name which at the time lacked luster, for he had not yet become the architect of a federated Europe and probably the best known Frenchman next to DeGaulle. When Hazard returned to the office he remembered saying to a colleague: "The British Empire is being saved by two Canadians and a Frenchman." This seemed astonishing in its implications, and to this day it is not clear what role Monnet was playing.

Since the Soviets were hard to please, their problems bounced from office to office. Dean Acheson, then Secretary of State, near the end of the war would call representatives of the various concerned governments to discuss the supply problems. On one occasion Lester Pearson was at his right hand. Pearson was of very quiet manners, and it was hard, from the worm's eye view, to sense his imagination and fire which he used later as Canadian Prime Minister to heal—or almost heal—the running dispute between French and English Canadians over the flag and over the language controversy.

Hazard kept the minutes of the Protocol Committee, a committee of representatives of all agencies, engaged in supplying the Soviets under the annual Protocol supply programs. He was privy to the struggle within the departments to protect their sources of materiel and to the expressions of concern from men who knew the importance of keeping the Soviets in the war, but who mistrusted their post-war aims. Perhaps the most impressive of the representatives was General Lucius Clay, later to become the United States Commissioner in defeated Germany. When the Soviet representatives asked for landing craft, Clay said: "No." He anticipated that they would use them on the Caspian Sea to move into Iran from which it would be hard later to dislodge them. Yet on some items, he was the major supporter. An enormous amount of copper field telephone wire was requested, so large that no one could see how it all could be used. Clay stepped right into the argument and, pointed out that vast amounts were, indeed, needed because every time the front changed, the entire system had to be left behind and new network set up at a new location. He supported the entire request, and it went through the committee.

Perhaps the most exciting moment came—at least with the advantage of hindsight—when the Soviet Purchasing Committee asked for heavy water and uranium. None of the clearance officers knew at that time what part these substances were to play in research on the atomic bomb. The Manhattan Project was still a total secret to the staff. By that time the Director of the U.S.S.R. branch had become Major General Charles M. Wesson, and Hazard remained as his Deputy Director. General Wesson knew something of the project, but he kept his mouth shut. When the yellow request sheets arrived from the Soviet Purchasing Commission as a routine request, procedure called for referral by the receiving officer to the desk that specialized in that category of goods. The officer would telephone to the department of government concerned with supply to make certain that the item was available, and then refer the matter to the full group at its morning meeting to determine whether any other officer, by chance, had information on the item that was relevant. If the item was on the protocol supply list specifically, the checks were routine, but some items were listed only generically as: chemicals. These two requests were not on the protocol specifically, so they went through scrutiny. General Wesson told the supply officer concerned to check the uranium with General Groves of the Manhattan Project whom no one else knew. The officer, James P. Hoopes, did so, and Groves gave his approval of a license saying that he did not expect that any could be obtained. The Soviet officer specializing in the items was told that supply was unlikely, but he reappeared later and reported that it had been found in Canada and shipped.

Years after the war, the House of Representatives Unamerican Activities Committee, with the benefit of hindsight, became concerned with the clearance as a possibly traitorous act to help the U.S.S.R. make the atomic bomb. Hazard was called down to Washington, as the last surviving official in charge of the office since Wesson had died. Also called was Hoopes. One of the office routines was to require every clearance officer to maintain a diary on which he entered every caller in person, every telephone call, and everything that might seem relevant. Hoopes, like all the others, had kept his diary and was able to show the Congressional Committee his entry of the talk he had with General Groves. Until the entry was found, Groves denied having any recollection of their conversation, but when it was located, his memory was refreshed. He said that he had given clearance because he did not expect any source to be found and did so to see if any suppliers did have uranium for sale.

Hoopes was congratulated by the Committee for keeping the diary with such care, but Hazard was grilled in closed session during which he was interrogated at some length, not about the clearance which had been cleared up, but as to why he had gone to the U.S.S.R. to study law. McCarthy never attacked him directly, but others who were examined were asked why they knew John Hazard. Clearly, McCarthy thought Hazard was a danger, and his doubts were reflected in other branches of government, so much so that when Hazard requested a passport he was required to file an affidavit stating that he had never been a communist. Fortunately, Columbia University made its lawyer Leon Lipson, presently a professor at the Yale Law School, available to prepare the affidavit. He called upon some friends of long standing who were close to the Chief of the passport bureau, Mrs. Ripley, to put in a good word. With this support, the passport was issued, but the tar of four years at the Moscow Juridical Institute and five years in close relationship with the Soviet supply officers in the Lend-Lease work of the war was never quite washed out of some government officials' minds. To have been a specialist on anything Soviet, even under circumstances as straight forward as those presented by the Institute of Current World's Fellowship and by the Lend-Lease program, raised suspicions in the McCarthy era of the 1950's.

Hazard had anticipated a Congressional investigation of Lend-Lease after the war because he knew that the wartime alliance would turn sour when the Soviets regained their strength and began again to press their cause throughout the world. On one occasion General Burns asked, "What will the Russians be like if we win?" Hazard replied, "They will be ornery and make life for the U.S.A. impossible." Because of that expectation, the Lend-Lease office kept voluminous files so that no Lend-Lease program was recorded better. The files were sent to the National Archives, where they remain and have provided material for several scholarly books upon the topic.

In view of this expectation of trouble later on, Hazard wanted to avoid any direct responsibility for final decisions. He imagined that a career of study in the U.S.S.R. would excite suspicions even though the auspices of his relationship to the Soviets were clearly to the benefit of American business and government. The problem was finding a Chief of the U.S.S.R. Branch to whom he could be comfortably made a deputy. As has been indicated, the first chief, Faymonville, and the second, Spalding, were chosen by Burns and outside Hazard's influence. But after Spalding was sent to Moscow to replace Faymonville who had angered the United States Embassy staff with his direct communication with Hopkins thereby shortcutting the Department of State, there was a choice.

Stettinius called in Hazard after an interval following Spalding's transfer and talked over the matter of electing the Chief. Hazard said immediately that he did not want to step up. He argued that some senior who had the full confidence of official Washington and of the White House was needed. He proposed Reeve Schley. Schley had just retired from a career as Vice-President of the Chase Bank. Even before recognition in 1933, he had protected the U.S.S.R. account from those who sought to attach it to cover claims they had against one or another Soviet firm. He had organized the American-Russian Chamber of Commerce which represented those American firms who were selling in the U.S.S.R. He had an office in Moscow while Hazard was a student, and they had become friends, strengthened by the fact that Schley was a senior member of Hazard's Yale Society. He was very well known to the Eastern Establishment, and Stettinius readily agreed to his nomination.

A few days later Schley was to pass through Washington on the train headed for the South, and Hazard went to the station to talk to him. He found Schley among the green curtains of the Pullman sleeping cars. It took very little coaxing to persuade him that the task of heading the U.S.S.R. Division in Lend-Lease would be a form of war service, and that with his long service to the benefit of American business and the Russians, he would be acceptable to all. Perhaps he was also persuaded by the fact that his wife thought a term in Washington would be exhilarating as a hostess. Whatever the motives, Schley came down within a short time, bought an attractive house in Georgetown and assumed the all-important responsibility for the program. He relied totally on the existing staff, made no changes, but served as a pillar of strength for the group of program officers Hazard had gathered around him from among old college friends in whom he had complete confidence.

Maxim Litvinov had by this time arrived as Ambassador. It was he who had met with Roosevelt in 1933 to arrange the reopening of diplomatic relations. He had brought the U.S.S.R. into the League of Nations in 1934. His revolutionary past was either unknown by most Americans or ignored. He was simply accepted as a top Soviet diplomat with whom a pragmatic relationship was possible. He took his place in the old Embassy building on 16th street and met with Schley and Hazard whenever a crisis arose over the progress of the supply program.

Although Litvinov was on hand, most of the daily routines went through the Soviet Government Purchasing Commission. This institution owed its structural form primarily to Stettinius. When Lend-Lease was begun in 1941, the Soviet government had conducted its trade through the Amtorg Trading Corporation in New York. This had been formed during the years of non-recognition so as to provide a trading mechanism apart from the Soviet government which had no status in the courts of the United States. One of Roosevelt's former classmates who served as counsel to Soviet trading interests had hit upon the idea of creating a New York corporation to be owned by a Soviet citizen. This would make it subject to New York law, and there would be no problem of non-recognition of governments or of pleas of immunity when recognition might be accorded.

It was Amtorg that assumed the duty of representing the U.S.S.R.'s commercial interests and of presenting requests to Lend-Lease when the program was initiated. Stettinius found in talking with government agencies that Amtorg retained its commercial mentality. Its commodity specialists took their time about making decisions. They haggled over the prices charged against their Lend-Lease account as shipments were made. They insisted upon minute inspection of items to be shipped, verifying every spare part down to the flashlight on a fighter plane. Stettinius was told that what was needed was not a merchant mentality but a military supply mentality which focused attention on quick deliveries, even with some shortcomings. He presented his request for a change to Litvinov and within a short time he was informed that the proposal had been accepted.

Hazard knew that for years the Soviet diplomats had hoped to establish a State Trading Delegation alongside their Embassy, as they had done in other countries. This had been resisted even at the time of recognition, because pleas of immunity were feared by the merchant community. Now the door was opened unexpectedly by the Americans themselves, and, of course, the Soviet government was happy to oblige. Within a short time Major General Belaev of the Soviet Air Force arrived to head the new Soviet Government Purchasing Commission. Upon his arrival he told Hazard that the greatest surprise of his life was when Britain and the United States offered, after the German attack of June 1941, to help the Soviet Government. He had always expected the imperialist powers to refuse aid in expectation that the hated Bolsheviks would go down to defeat.

Most of his staff was transferred from the Amtorg Trading Corporation, including the Amtorg's President, Lukashev who had once been Rector of the University of Leningrad and a world-renowned specialist on permanently frozen Arctic soil. As he once lamented, he had been sent to New York to head Amtorg and taken away from his beloved science. He saw it as a personal tragedy but one that had to be born as a Communist Party member sworn to accept discipline. In spite of the carryover from Amtorg, supply arrangements were speeded along with Belaev's arrival. Only after the war, when Dean Acheson as Secretary of State asked the Soviet Government and all other governments having supply missions to close them in accordance with American policy to discourage state trading, did chickens come home to roost. For the Soviet diplomats this was retrogression, for they thought their Supply Mission the obvious forerunner of a standard State Trading Delegation.

They made this clear to Hazard as soon as their Embassy received Secretary Acheson's note, since he had made a mistake in handling the papers. Under State Department procedures, every document prepared for transmission to a foreign government contained the drafting officer's initials on the third and subsequent drafts. Only the original and one courtesy copy were blind. Hazard by that time had been named Adviser on State Trading in the Commercial Policy division of the Department of State, and it was his task to draft Acheson's letter. What happened was this: Acheson had all copies on his desk. When the Soviet Embassy official called upon him he picked up the original and the third copy with JNH typed upon it. It took the Purchasing Commission only a few hours to learn who had prepared the letter, and their man was in Hazard's office telling him that they now knew who their enemy was. To them, the whole close-out was Hazard's doing, and they would not listen to the explanation that the British and all the others had received the same letter since it was long established U.S. policy to oppose state trading.

Schley's health began to fail after two years, and a replacement was needed. By this time the Lend-Lease program had been transferred to the Board of Economic Warfare for administrative purposes, although it remained close to the White House. The choice of the Administrator was the retired Chief of Ordinance, Major General Charles M. Wesson, fondly known as "Bull" for his pugnaciousness. He came down in his full uniform covered with the usual service ribbons and added military luster to relations with the Lieutenant General Rudenko who had replaced Belaev at the Soviet Government Purchasing Commission.

Wesson proved to be a kindly man in spite of his nickname. Like Schley he was content to utilize the staff exactly as he found it. He insisted on no replacements by cronies of long standing. He kept Hazard on as his deputy and relied on him for every detail of administration, saying only on his first day at his desk: "Hazard, there is only one rule around here—absolute loyalty!" There was never a "leak" from that U.S.S.R. Branch, and Wesson had his loyalty right up to the end of the war and the termination of Lend-Lease. Although Hazard had his doubts about the wisdom of the abrupt termination of the program when Wesson recommended to Leo Crowley, the Administrator at the time, that the program end as the war had been won, he did not speak out. There was no negotiation, as one might have expected. The axe simply fell, and was to give historians in subsequent decades a question to debate: Was Lend-Lease's abrupt termination, even to the point of turning vessels around at sea, a cause of the post-war tensions leading eventually to the cold war?

Hazard had been telling the specialists of the Soviet Government Purchasing Commission throughout the war that they must appreciate that Lend-Lease was accorded not because the U.S. government had changed its views on the Soviet Union's system of government but because it was necessary to save the United States itself. General Burns had been talking in these terms ever since the early days when Hopkins and Harriman decided that supplies must go forward even if Stalin would not supply information as the British did on what they had in their stocks. Burns continued throughout the war to serve as a goad in the supply program for the U.S.S.R., and he was not relieved when his Division of Defense Aid Reports was absorbed in the Lend-Lease Administration. He was simply moved over to the half-empty marble building of the Federal Reserve Bank and from that office, to which Colonel William MacChesney Martin was assigned as a deputy, he continued to supervise the program from afar without any clear line of command authority. Hazard saw him often, and found in him a wise counselor when things went wrong, bringing the Soviet officials into the office to complain in their inimitable fashion.

Long years of working with Soviet citizens had taught Hazard something about how to maintain relationships. He tried to be friendly but firm when a decision had to be communicated to them. The Soviet officials would arrange lunches or dinners for their American counterparts, at which they sought or gave favors. Hazard tried to explain to his own staff and to those in the War Production Board, who had to clear Soviet civilian supplies, that dinners were not compliments; they were ways of extracting favors. He even applied a rule of thumb: Conversation at a meal would be about anything until the dessert. Then came the matter that was on Soviet minds, and it became clear why the invitation was issued. Favors went beyond meals: The Soviet commission gave gifts. A general rule was established that no clearance officer on the staff could accept anything but a small gift of produce that could be eaten or drunk, or perhaps a record of some Soviet music. Even Stettinius was plied with gifts and on one occasion he found it necessary to return a silver tea service which was brought to him at Christmas. As far as Hazard knew, no staff member was ever offered money, and no gifts were accepted that could be considered more than what might be presented to a hostess after a weekend in the country.

In subsequent years it became commonplace to say that Roosevelt and Hopkins gave away a great deal unnecessarily because the United States was never in danger. At the time, it did not look that way. Burns once told Hazard that the German submarines were sinking supply ships faster than Kaiser could build them in his shipyards. Before the battle of Stalingrad he commented on the fact that with the Japanese crossing Burma toward India, and the German armies advancing to the Volga, it was quite possible that they would eventually meet in Iran and close the noose around the U.S.S.R. The United States would have to fight with its weakened British ally or retreat to its continental fortress, and hope that a satiated Hitler would leave it alone. Historians now report that documents prove Hitler had ambitions to rule the world. Absurd as it now seems, the wartime years were fearful years for those in Washington, and Roosevelt passed on the word that the U.S.S.R. must be kept in the war. There must not be another Rapallo like that after the First World War when Germans and Russians buried the hatchet and chose to work together. The men and women far down the line in Hazard's office believed what they were told. They thought their task critical.

Chapter Six
WITH THE VICE-PRESIDENT

WITH THE VICE-PRESIDENT

It was May 21, 1944 and America's largest four-engine transport plane was warming up on the tarmak at the Washington military airport. The Vice-President of the United States was about to fly off to China on a secret mission set by President Roosevelt. The plan was to persuade Chiang Kai-shek and the communists to unite their efforts to defeat the Japanese Imperial Army.

Henry Wallace had been planning his trip for weeks. A group of specialists in the countries he was to visit had been assembled: John Carter Vincent as the principal aide for the Chinese portion of the trip, Owen Lattimore, the noted specialist on Mongolia for the Mongolian interlude, and Hazard for the section of the flight that would go through the U.S.S.R. Hazard had been brought into the group by Faymonville, who on his return from Moscow's Lend-Lease office had been keeping in touch with Wallace. Indeed the Soviet segment of the trip was Faymonville's work. It was he who plotted the places on the map that he wanted visited.

Wallace was ready himself for the Soviet segment: He had been studying the Russian language for months, and he had prepared some speeches with the help of his tutor. They were to be in Russian and given along the way through Siberia. He had asked Roosevelt for permission to linger in the U.S.S.R. on the way to China, and the permission had been granted. The Department of State then negotiated the details with their colleagues in the Soviet foreign office. But there was one fly in the ointment, namely Averell Harriman, who was at that time, the United States Ambassador in Moscow. He declared that Wallace must not fly into Moscow to see Stalin. Harriman had seen how high-level emissaries had undercut Ambassadors at their posts, and he was not going to be undercut. His years in politics had taught him how to play the political game so as not to lose his power. That meant that the Soviet segment of the trip would be touristic and nothing more. But a half a loaf was better than none, and Wallace accepted the limitation.

The plane flew northward across the United States and Canada to Alaska with a refueling stop at Edmonton. Fairbanks was the first major stop. The 24-hour day was almost upon the city by the time the party arrived. The route over which the plane was flying was the one used to deliver the fighter planes being sent to the Russians under Lend-Lease, so it was well-equipped for heavy traffic. Wallace inspected the installations, and then off he flew over Nome to Siberia. The passengers could see the ice-cakes as they went out over the heavy breakers on the Nome shoreline. They soon saw the Siberian side, particularly, a tiny place called Semchan. Siberian tundra looked bleak from the landing strip. The group was met by the official welcoming delegation, headed by a Georgian named Goglidze, said to be an intimate friend of Beria, the Soviet chief of the security police. But there were also two Foreign Office officials, Dmitri Chuvakhin who had served in the Soviet Embassy in Washington at an earlier time, and a protocol officer to make arrangements.

The little party was taken to a log-cabin type of building near the airport for the night, but sleep was preceded by a banquet such as only the Russians can provide: the cold zakuski, the hot zakuski, vodka, wines, fruits, and cakes. Wallace was an abstemious man. He never drank a drop of alcohol. He was also a light eater. He said early on, "John, tell them that all I want is a cheese sandwich." Hazard, with his experience with the Russians, knew that their pride would be hurt if they could not entertain as they had expected to do, and more importantly, the local officials who had not seen a good meal throughout the war would miss the opportunity of their lives. He pleaded with Wallace to let the show go on as it had been planned by the hosts. Wallace agreed, but he wanted to be sure that all he was offered was his cheese sandwich. The Soviet hosts agreed, so throughout the trip, he sat at the head of the table, as Soviet Protocol dictated, and the party sat on each side to stuff themselves with the dishes which looked for all the world like those to be obtained in a first class Moscow hotel.

Hazard wondered how the local people at that remote point in Siberia on the shores of the Bering Sea could have prepared such an impeccable meal. He wondered also how the buxom women who waited on them had been found, because it was common knowledge that Siberia was bereft of women, so much so that planeloads of candidates for marriage were flown out to the outposts from time to time. One woman confided to him that most of the women tried to get off at the early stops on their way Eastward, so that they would not be relegated to the remote places. He got his lesson in management at the next stopping place, for the same head waiter and waitresses appeared at that stop. He expressed surprise to the head waiter, who casually replied that the entire team had been brought from Moscow, and each evening after serving dinner, they would climb with their equipment and supplies into planes to move on to be ready at the next stop.

The party flew westward across Siberia, but first there were stops in the Far East. The party was flown to Komsomolsk which was the town built by young communists in the early years after the revolution to open up the Far East. It was a youthful town, for only hardy young Komsomols had been the settlers. It seemed to have more children in the community than the party had ever seen before. It showed off its crèches and factories. The party was especially interested in whether the much-talked-of Amur Baikal railroad had been finished. It was to provide an alternate route farther north to the Trans-Siberian railroad, which was the achilles heel of Soviet Far Eastern military activity. From the plane the graded railroad bed leading into the city from the West could be seen, but it was not clear how far to the West it went. Actually, the railroad had not yet been completed by the 1980's, although work was progressing.

The conversations along the way gave Hazard a chance to check on what had been happening to the Lend-Lease supplies which had been sent across the Pacific from Seattle to the Soviet port of Magadan behind the Kuriles. The plane stopped also at that port. It was famous among American specialists as the place to which great numbers of exiles had been sent by the security police to serve their terms in the gold fields of Siberia. On the docks were the piles of crates of Lend-Lease equipment waiting for transit to the interior. The party was taken to the gold fields, where Lend-Lease shovels were evident. The huge Bucyrus Erie machines were not supposed to be put to work on gold, but there they were, within the barbed wire enclosures of the prison camps. Lined up beside them were men who were portrayed as prisoners, dressed in their blue jeans.

Critics of the Wallace trip have since said that these workers were really not the prisoners, who were obviously in the camps, but security police guards dressed up for the occasion. This may have been so, but the party did not think of this element of drama at the time. One evening the mayor of the city, or rather the commander, for he was a high officer of the MVD who ruled the detention town, invited the party to the music hall to see the nineteenth century light opera with which the Russians amused themselves throughout the country. During the intermission, the group paraded around the foyer in typical Soviet style, finding themselves among well-dressed women and officers. Hazard asked the commander how they happened to have so many of the intelligentsia at such a remote place. His reply was simply, "We ought to have some very good people, for these are the exiles from Leningrad." There was no effort to conceal the fact that Magadan was a place of exile beyond any possibility of escape through the forests of Siberia. Exiles were not only the poor fellows condemned to work in the gold fields, or on the docks, but the intelligentsia who had their usual jobs as office staff, teachers, musicians, artists, shop clerks, being free to move about but limited to the confines of the city.

Wallace talked endlessly with the host group, who had been ordered, evidently, to be genial. When Russians at the official level have orders, they obey, and geniality can be very pleasant, although those who have lived in the U.S.S.R. know that the switch can be turned, and unpleasantness can replace geniality in a moment. One of his own interesting companions in the plane was the MVD colonel assigned to protect Wallace. He was dressed in his uniform and always wore white gloves. He had served with the Cheka after the revolution, and the GPU, and was now with its successor, the MVD. He bore on his chest the jubilee medal honoring him for this service. He was a man of polished manners, no brutish type, whatever his tasks had been over the years. Hazard knew that everything the party did was being watched and reported and that there was no way to keep things secret. He arranged with the Colonel to help in the preparation of the daily telegram to Roosevelt on what was going on. The Colonel seemed to relish the opportunity to put it in impeccable Russian and to see that it went off in some kind of code to America.

Years later Hazard's Columbia colleague Willis Reese confided that during the war he had been reading the Japanese reports of the trip as they were decoded, and that he found the constant references to a certain "Hazardu" as he moved with Wallace across Siberia. The experience only confirmed Hazard's long-time impression that everything one does when in the public eye, and often as a private citizen, is known to those who need to know. He has marvelled in the revelations following nominations to government positions of prominent people at how many of them are amazed to find turned up in their records events which they thought would never surface. Out of this experience, Hazard has always told students that they live in a goldfish bowl, and the sooner they appreciate that fact, the better for their career.

The Colonel of the MVD figured in one extraordinary event that occurred on the Yenesei river during an excursion out of Krasnoyarsk. Hazard had suggested to Wallace that he ought to have a ride on a river boat on a Siberian river. Hazard had been down the Volga on such a boat a couple of times, and he recalled the view that the traveler had of a life rather like that of Mark Twain on the Mississippi. Wallace jumped at the proposal, and it was made to Goglidze. He reported back a couple of days later that the trip would occur at Krasnoyarsk, and sure enough when the party reached that new industrial city, they were told that the boat would be ready in the morning.

When the party reached the river wharf, Hazard was disappointed that the boat had no other passengers. It had obviously been taken off its regular run and reserved for the Wallace party alone. The Mark Twain effects would, therefore, be missing. Still, it could be a pretty trip, and fortunately of some value to him as a source of information because the top Communist Party Secretary of the Province was to be on board. As the boat jiggled its way south up the river toward its source, Hazard engaged the party man in conversation. He asked naively, "How do you choose the members of the Provincial delegation to the meetings of the Supreme Soviet?" The reply was seemingly honest, "We take the nominations that come up to us from meetings in the various nominating groups in farms, factories, Universities and so on; we discuss within the Party which are the most active and politically conscious people; we then consider what kind of distribution we want to represent the Province; we know we must have some collective farmers, some simple workmen, some very old people, some actors and writers to show off our intelligentsia, some Party officials, and some of the officials from the soviet apparatus. Then we choose from our list of approved nominees which people meet this scheme, and assign them to the various voting districts to be voted on." Hazard knew that with the one-candidate ballot, the choices would be formally elected without question, and he could see that this was a sort of planned representation. His host saw that too, for he added, "We think this better representation than your system where most of your members of Congress are lawyers."

During the early afternoon Wallace said he needed to walk. Wallace was not only a teatotaler, and a cheese sandwich eater; he was determined to have his daily exercise. At every stop in Siberia, it was arranged for him to play volleyball with a team from the local garrison and with the crew of his own airplane. His exercise program had caught his hosts' imagination, and they seemed to enjoy arranging things to meet his needs. When Hazard told Goglidze that Wallace wanted to walk on the shore, Goglidze went to the bridge, and shortly the anchors from bow and stern were tossed onto the banks and the ship brought alongside the meadow at the foot of the local mountain. Wallace hurried ashore, followed by Hazard and the MVD Colonel. Wallace looked at the mountain covered by thick forest not yet in leaf. "Let's go up," he said, and off he started. Hazard and the Colonel rushed along behind.

Wallace had good wind, and raced ahead. The aging Colonel found the going too heavy, and he suggested slowing down, but Hazard knew Wallace would not do so. He urged the Colonel to wait along the way, while he and Wallace continued. The Colonel acquiesced, thinking possibly, that Hazard was his counterpart, a secret police operator assigned to protect Wallace on the trip. Little did he know that Hazard had no knowledge even of how to use a revolver, being trained with a specialization in the routines of the law. So the Colonel sat down in the forest, and his famous charge went on.

Hazard followed the boy scout routine of putting twigs in the trees as they plunged along. There was no trail at all. He feared they might be lost on the mountain. Finally, even he, young as he was, tired, and he told Wallace he would have to rest. Wallace kept on alone. Presumably, he would tire at some point and turn back to pass and pick up Hazard and the Colonel. So they both waited at their respective resting spots in the forest. Time passed, and there was no sign of Wallace. The Colonel called up from below, "Gde Vis-President?" Hazard could only reply "Nye znaiou." Finally, he decided that he must descend and tell the crew on the ship that the Vice-President of the United States was missing in the forests of Siberia. He could see the headlines in the *New York Times,* "VICE-PRESIDENT LOST." He knew what this would mean for the Colonel: He might even be executed by Stalin. For himself, there could be no such fate, but it would have been an unhappy moment in his life, to put it mildly!

There was nothing to do but descend. He followed the twig marked path to the Colonel, and then they went straight down to the boat. As they came out of the forest to the meadow, they could see Wallace playing horseshoes with his crewmates. He seemed unperturbed. He just looked up as if he had expected Hazard and the Colonel to come along at some time. He made no apologies: They just went back on board, turned the ship around, and sailed north in the late afternoon sun. They could see the lighthouse buoy keepers rowing out at intervals to light the navigation lamps along the way as shadows fell.

Wallace was an agricultural wizard. He had developed hybrid corn, and was busily working on other hybrids in his spare time. He had once been Secretary of Agriculture before becoming Vice-President, and before that he had been the editor of a noted farm journal. He had asked his hosts before leaving America for an opportunity to see their agricultural experiment stations. He had read about the famous Lysenko claim that environment could change plant characteristics and that these characteristics could be inherited. As a noted geneticist he did not believe it. He also knew that the famous Soviet geneticist Vavilov had been removed from his genetic laboratory and might have been executed. Genetics was an ugly word in Stalin's vocabulary at the time. This whetted Wallace's appetite for a look at what was really happening in the experiment stations.

The party went to several, the most memorable being one in which work was being done with alfalfa. Wallace knew a lot about that plant, and he was intensely interested. He was pleased with what he saw and told Goglidze that the head man was one of the best researchers he had seen. Later on in the trip Goglidze told Hazard to tell Wallace that the man had been decorated with the Order of Lenin on Wallace's recommendation. On one memorable evening in Irkutsk, after a day floating on Lake Baikal, Wallace asked if he might meet with the faculty of the Irkutsk University. They were gathered by the Rector in a large room, and the questions began. It was the most difficult interpreting Hazard had ever done, for he was not a scientist. He stumbled along, but it seemed that his help was hardly needed. Scientists are so international that both the Soviet professors and Wallace seemed to know what was being said before the translation was made.

At the very end, Wallace asked Hazard to request that someone from the medical faculty come up to talk with him. When the doctor reached the front of the room, Wallace said he had stomach pains. There was consternation among the hosts. He was hurried back to the guesthouse at the edge of Irkutsk where the party was staying, and a medical delegation of nine doctors arrived to examine him. They concluded that it was only indigestion, but they wrote out a protocol with the diagnosis and all nine signed it. It was clear that if the Vice-President were to die, no single man could be charged with killing him or failing to diagnose his ailment properly. One of their number was left on the spot to be available throughout the night.

Wallace looked at the pile of black powder that was put before him as medicine. He sniffed it, tasted it and said to Hazard, "This is just charcoal, like the medicine my grandmother used to give me in Kansas when I was a boy." He felt safe with it, and swallowed the dose. By the next morning he was well again, and the crisis that had been feared was over.

The wooden guesthouse at Irkutsk was one of many in which the party stayed. Indeed, they never went to an ordinary hotel. It seemed that in every town there was a guesthouse set aside for the top government official who would be coming through from time to time on inspection trips. Wallace was being put in those houses. They were usually in a forest patch on the edge of town, well away from the general public. This insulated the party from the people, which displeased Wallace, but he was a guest and could not ask for a change. On one occasion, he got a taste of the hard life, for one apartment, with overstuffed furniture, proved to be in the old Russian tradition which Hazard had come to know as a student in Moscow. When the party turned off the lights to sleep, it was only a short time before the biting began. Hazard knew the symptoms, "bedbugs." He jumped up to switch on the lights, and there they were, coming out of the stuffing in the furniture.

Fortunately the party had been supplied by the air force before leaving with a newly developed aerosol bomb containing the newly discovered DDT. No one then knew how dangerous it was to humans. The party members just dropped their pajamas and sprayed themselves with DDT as if it were water. It stopped the bedbugs, although it may have put poison into their systems, to appear decades later. This seems not to have happened, for Wallace lived to a ripe old age, and the other members of the party seem to be having the same luck.

Finally, at Alma Ata, the party was to say good-bye. They saw a performance of *Carmen* at the local opera house. Carmen was sung by a Central Asia woman with a high, nasal voice. She sang the familiar Bizet arias just as if she were being accompanied with a one string fiddle and a flute. It was excruciatingly painful to Western ears, but the party sat it out and marvelled at what each culture takes to be a beautiful tone.

On that last day, Wallace, in chatting with Chuvakhin, asked what denomination he would be were he to become a religious believer. Chuvakhin did not hesitate. He replied, "Roman Catholic, of course." Wallace was a staunch protestant, and he said to Hazard, "John, I would have expected that. Dmitri likes discipline; he likes to have confidence in his faith. Catholicism and Communism have much in common."

Wallace had another remarkable observation following his experience in Siberia and Central Asia. It came from watching Goglidze and the traveling group of servants who accompanied the party. He said to Hazard, "John, these people mistreat their servants. I do not like it." That brief summation, of what everyone who has lived in the U.S.S.R. knows to be true, would have been an answer to many Americans who thought Wallace to be a "communist." He was not. He was a simple democratic American with a warm heart, who thought the lucky people in this world should share some of their wealth with the downtrodden and the poor.

With a farewell wave to the Soviet hosts, the party boarded their plane to fly along the Ili River valley into the Sinkiang Province of China. They would be met at its capital, Urumchi, by a delegation from Chiang Kai-shek sent up to greet them. Also at the foot of the gangplank, was the United States Consul in the city, one Oliver Clubb. He was later to be tarred by the brush of the McCarthyites as one of the causes of China's turn to communism, along with the rest of a number of Department of State China specialists, including John Carter Vincent, who was now to take over from Hazard as interpreter and confidant of the Vice-President. Wallace told Hazard simply, "John, you can now go to the back of the plane. Send up John Carter. You are through."

Because he was through, Hazard expected no one to welcome him in Urumchi. He waited a respectful period of time after Wallace descended the stairs to meet the Governor and his party, and then he went out with the plane's crew to be taken wherever the supporting staff was to be quartered. At the bottom of the stairs stood a dignified scholar in his long black high-collared gown. He stepped forward. "Are you Dr. Hazard? I have the honor to escort you." It seemed clear that this specialist on communism was not going to be left to wander around in Kuomintang China on his own. That night Hazard slept behind the crenelated walls of the fortress in which the governor's palace sat. He watched the sentry pacing them, as a sentry must have done for centuries past as merchants traveled along the silk route from the Orient to the West. Marco Polo may have passed that way.

Wallace was to visit the Chinese experiment stations where many of the agronomists in charge spoke English. They were graduates of the famous Cornell faculty. He felt right at home. He played volleyball every afternoon with groups assigned by the Army, just as he had in the U.S.S.R. He crossed over the Gobi desert in all its threatening majesty and over the Great Wall, which seemed to be the exact barrier between the desert and the fertile paddy fields of the peasants. Soon they descended to Chungking where Chiang Kai-shek made his capital. Once again a delegation was at the plane, and off the party went to the Generalissimo's home in the suburbs. This time Hazard was not left behind, but taken along with the rest.

When they reached the big house, Mme. Chiang was there to greet Wallace. He and John Carter Vincent would stay with her in the big house. Hazard would sleep with Owen Lattimore in a cottage in the garden. He repaired to it immediately with a strong feeling of fatigue. The garden cottage might have been in England. It was charming in Western style, and it even had a full bathroom. Hazard thought a bath would relax him for a nap. He turned on the faucet in the tub. No water came out, but he heard a racket outside: many excited voices, and laughter. He looked out the window: There was a group of coolies with a brazier, a water bucket and two funnels in front of them leading to the pipes which ended in the bathtub. The cottage had running water, but the running feature was provided by the coolies. Here was modern and ancient China in one operation.

Dinner was served in the big house. The Generalissimo sat at one end of the table and his wife at the other. The host said almost nothing for John Carter Vincent to interpret. Mme. Chiang did the talking. She was a Wellesley girl through and through, with a perfect American cultured accent, a charm that was engaging, and a sense of humor quite like that of a gentlewoman in the United States. It was totally disarming. On later occasions, when the party lingered at the table, Hazard lost sight of the fact that she was the ears of the Generalissimo. Had he known any state secrets, he would have been induced to divulge them as he might have done in confidence to a sister. Mme. Chiang was a charmer. At the time, she was in her early forties, and a beauty, really irresistible. After this first dinner, Chiang excused himself early, saying through John Carter that he must return to the Operations Room along side to continue with the war.

What Wallace said to Chiang Hazard has never known. John Carter was the only one present with Wallace at the official meetings, which had been the purpose of the long trip. Lattimore and Hazard were turned over to the guides. Wallace gave him only one assignment, "John, you go to the Soviet Embassy, for I want them not to feel left out." The Protocol officer provided the car with a chauffer and "footman" in white uniform to take him over. He was met at the door by the Counselor. He had been briefed by the Embassy to know that the Ambassador was himself a noted specialist on China and was even reputed to write Chinese poetry.

The conversation with the Ambassador and the Counselor was inconsequential; just a recounting of the events of the trip and expressions from Hazard of how much Wallace had appreciated the hospitality. He had arrived in mid-morning. At noon he rose to leave but the Ambassador said the staff would shortly be going in to luncheon and would not Gospodin Hazard remain? Hazard said that the President's car was below and might be needed, but the Ambassador said he would have the President's office informed of the change in plans, so Hazard stayed. The staff came in, and they all sat down to a solid Russian meal of borsch, kasha and lamb. The table gossip was light and full of fun. Russians can be full of fun when not required to be serious. Nothing of consequence occurred, but one can be sure that the whole affair was reported back to Moscow, and Wallace's goodwill measured by the fact that he had arranged the meeting.

At the end of the visit to Chungking, there was one of the usual Chinese banquets. The main course was ham, the explanation being that it was easier to serve a western meal than a Chinese one. Hazard was thrilled to find that he had been seated next to Mme. Sun Yat-sen, sister of Mme. Chiang. She was a polished speaker in English, and although not as beautiful as her sister, a charming person—not yet the mountain of a woman she was to become in the 1970's as one of the Vice-President's of the People's Republic. The conversation was about the trip through Siberia and Hazard's schooling in Moscow. There was no political message from either side. She did at one point indicate that down the table on the far side sat Chou En-lai, who was the Communist's emissary at the office of Chiang. This was the man Wallace was trying to bring closer to Chiang so that a united front against the Japanese would become a reality. The mission had no evident success along these lines.

Hazard saw something of the city with his guides, visited some schools, and the waterfront on the great river. He had one of his teeth fixed by a U.S. Army dentist stationed with the troops.

The party left by plane for cities farther south. Wallace wanted to see Stillwell's headquarters in Kunming, the new name for the ancient city of Yunan-fu. Hazard looked back in memory as they flew, to his jungle trip years earlier with Harold Young, to visit his mission in the westernmost corner of that province facing Burma.

The city was a typical, crowded Chinese hill town, with masses of people in narrow streets, so full that the cars with the official party could scarcely get through. The high point was to be a dinner at the Governor's palace on the highest hill, and the party was driven up to it, through rows of guards. The Governor was said to be an old-fashioned warlord who ran his own show, and gave little heed to what Chungking wanted. Still, the party was now accompanied by Mme. Chiang's brother, T.V. Soong, who was nominally Foreign Minister, and formal acceptance of central authority seemed to be in order.

"T.V." took the party to see a light arms factory, which was pitifully small. He bemoaned the fact that "China has no raw materials to make arms." What a contrast this shop was to what Mao later developed in China when the minerals were found! Hazard stayed with John Davies in his billet, and ate some of his meals with Joseph Alsop, who was Stillwell's public relations man. Davies was later to be criticized as the arch-enemy of America and the one who played a large part in subverting Chiang's system. It took years before he was exonerated. Alsop became one of America's most widely read columnists. On the road to the General's quarters, the party passed a long file of soldiers marching to one knew not where. They looked exhausted, and some were carrying stretchers bearing those of their comrades too sick to walk. It was a quick but telling glimpse of the state of the Generalissimo's armies.

With whatever mission Wallace had to perform accomplished, the party headed back north to stop at Chengtu and Langcho. This was Genghis Khan country, and his tomb was in the suburbs of Langcho, but Hazard did not see it. He came down with a fever and asked if a doctor was to be had. He was thrilled to hear that an English missionary doctor lived in the town, and he received Hazard in the evening. He asked Hazard if he had any aspirin. He did, and the doctor prescribed it. For his fee, he indicated that he would like to have what remained as he could get no good Bayer aspirin. The next morning the fever had gone, but weakness remained. Hazard felt horribly ill as he stood with the party by the plane to hear the long Chinese national anthem played by the band. But he did not faint; he climbed the stairs to the plane and off they went to Outer Mongolia, across the desolate sands of the Gobi. As the hours passed, his strength returned. He looked down upon the camel tracks in the sand until the frontier had been passed and the grasslands of Mongolia came in sight.

They landed in Ulan Bator and were met by the legendary Choi Balsang, the Lenin of the Mongolian communist revolution. He was surrounded by his colleagues, all dressed in brightly colored Chinese silk ankle-length robes. This was Mongolia, made a little odd by the fact that on each head was a western-style felt hat. The party was placed in cars and they traveled across the grasslands. They passed sheep herds which grazed on the hillsides. Near the edge of town, the cars turned right to go up a valley, and there were the yurts. These were the largest ones Hazard had seen. They were the guest colony for the visitors.

The party was assigned two by two to yurts; Wallace, however, had his own. Hazard was with Lattimore again. He entered the yurt first and heard a buzzing like a hive of bees. He jumped back in alarm, but saw that the noise came from a huge blue dragonpatterned crock under the central hole in the top of the yurt. It was covered with cheese cloth. He looked in and there was mare's milk fermenting wildly.

Lattimore soon came in, heard the sound, rushed over, exclaimed with joy, dipped in a small blue bowl and swallowed the milk. He had spent his boyhood among the Mongols, and knew the language perfectly, and relished the "komys," as it was called. Thus began a truly unusual visit, for few foreigners had visited Mongolia since it allied itself with the U.S.S.R. Lattimore now was the interpreter, and he was fascinating. There were few such experts in the world, and he was well-known to the Mongols. They thought him to be a friend of their culture. Wallace had no evident "business" to conduct in Ulan Bator. He was just a tourist as he had been in Siberia, but he was treated like an honored guest. He gave Choi Balsan two university laboratory type student microscopes. Hazard had selected them in Washington as a suitable gift for a developing country establishing its first University. The microscopes had engraved brass plaques upon them "From the People of the United States to the People of Mongolia." One wonders whether the plaques are still in place and whether students see them as they conduct their studies in the laboratory of the University.

On the day they were to leave, the weather was ominous. Colonel Kite, the pilot, said he did not know if he could get through to Siberia, for the front was a thick one. Still, he started off, and everyone said goodbye; but when he got north he decided he could not get through. He would have to return. Wallace was, of course, embarrassed. He asked the Colonel to wireless back that the return would be an unofficial visit. There were to be no ceremonies. When the plane came in for a landing on the grassland of the airport (there was no concrete), it bounced to a stop at the terminal. The Minister of Agriculture was there in his long silk purple robe and his western felt hat. He took the party back to the yurts.

Fortunately for Hazard, the return visit was an extra dividend, for the Minister of Agriculture spoke Russian. He had studied agronomy in the U.S.S.R. At dinner that evening, as the party ate lamb entrails stuffed with cornmeal, he and Hazard conversed about the Soviet and American federal systems. The Mongolian said that he had studied both, and he thought the Soviet one a more desirable system because the Republics of the Soviet federation were permitted to secede. He noted that in the United States. no secession was possible, and a civil war had been fought to prevent it. If only Henry Clay had been there to hear him! Of course it would have been ineffective to note that Stalin had stated on several occasions that there could be no turning back to an independence for the Republics. That would lead to a return to capitalism, and the communist party would struggle against any such movement. One could only sit and wonder if the argument indicated that Mongolia was thinking of joining the U.S.S.R., with the expectation that it could secede if it found the choice in error. At least, to date, there has been no move in that direction, so perhaps the Minister was just pulling the leg of his guest.

The plane got through on the second try, and was back in the U.S.S.R. for a night of rest before flying off to Alaska for the Fourth of July. It was sunsetless weather, and the party played baseball at midnight. They visited the University of Alaska's agricultural projects, where Wallace received the press. The first thing he heard was that Roosevelt had dropped him as his running mate in the next campaign. Harry Truman had been chosen instead. It was a blow to Wallace. He retreated into his shell. We of his staff wondered whether Roosevelt had sent him on a "mission" to get him out of the country while arrangements were made to drop him. In any event his career in the public eye was over. He went back to his farm to develop a new line of strawberries, and his colleagues went back to a more prosaic life.

Chapter Seven
DRAFTING THE NUREMBERG INDICTMENT

DRAFTING THE NUREMBERG INDICTMENT

The war was grinding to a close. The Nazi leaders were either dead or in prison. The Western leaders were considering what should be done in that early summer of 1945. Many wanted a court martial and speedy execution of Goering and his comrades-in-arms. Others saw the opportunity to make new international law. The Kellogg-Briand Peace Pact of 1924 had declared war to be illegal as an instrument of foreign policy, but there was, as yet, no clear statement that waging aggressive war was a crime. There was nothing whatever that even suggested that the leaders of a nation that mistreated individuals, as Hitler had mistreated the Jews and Gypsies, could be held accountable under international law to the rest of the world.

The governments of the allied powers finally concluded that this was a moment for a trial that would not be a court martial but something of more lasting effect; something that would be an historic milestone in the law. It was agreed that a trial would be held in Nuremberg at which the Nazi leaders would be brought before an International Tribunal composed of judges representing the four victorious powers: the United States, the United Kingdom, the U.S.S.R. and France. An indictment would be prepared in London setting forth the facts and the law that would be applied, and the trial would follow. The whole proceeding was expected to move along quickly. The four governments signed what was called "A Charter of the International Military Tribunal" on August 8, 1945 under which each signatory was to appoint a Prosecutor who would prepare for the trial.

President Truman asked Mr. Justice Robert Jackson to accept the post and to take leave from the United States Supreme Court where he was sitting. He had once been Attorney General of the United States and understood a prosecutor's task. Jackson was an organizer, and he quickly gathered around him a group of experts, not only on international law, but on the legal systems that would be of concern during the trial: the English, French, German and Soviet. Of course, he had his own vast knowledge of the system in use in the United States. Hazard was chosen as the expert on Soviet law. Jackson had been in touch with Hazard in earlier years because of his concern with the study of various legal systems. It was a time when the Lend-Lease program was slowing down, but it was still a long way from liquidation. It was a question of whether General Wesson would let his man Friday leave the office, but he agreed when General Burns said he would assign Colonel William

McChesney Martin to the temporary job of guiding the staff Hazard had built up.

Hazard was sent to London in August to assume his duties. Wartime arrangements still prevailed. Those who were to cross the Atlantic were sent to a staging point near New York and were kept under conditions of secrecy. Hazard's orders had been cut, and indicated that he was to have the simulated rank of "Major." He was to report to a military office in London, and was to assume duties as adviser to the U.S. Chief of Prosecution of Axis Criminality. Hazard reached the military base and signed in. He was told to wait until some point on some day when his name would be called on the loudspeakers of the base, and he was to be prepared to leave instantly. Meanwhile he could wander about the base and await the call. He did this until one late afternoon some days later, when he heard his name come out on the speakers. He went to the office, received a briefing on how to survive if the plane dropped into the sea, and soon the group was off in a military transport plane for Iceland.

After a refueling stop, the plane went on to Prestwick, Scotland where it was late at night on arrival. The airport car drove the officers and simulated officers up to an old mansion on the hill, in which long rows of iron cots had been placed in the great halls. Everyone was assigned a place among the sleeping soldiers. One wondered how safe money, passports, and valuables might be, but everyone was tired. Hazard hoped that the valuables under his pillow could not be sneaked out without arousing him. By early morning the mess call was heard, and everyone went down to receive their next orders. Hazard's called for immediate departure for London by plane. They were off on a typical Scotch-English day of scattered clouds, sunny moments, and space enough between the clouds to see the rolling countryside. Hazard knew it well from a number of earlier visits, especially the long motor ride with his Mother in the summer of 1929. It was thrilling to be back again. Everything looked so peaceful that one could hardly imagine that England had been through the hell of the "blitz."

In London, the reception officer said Hazard was to stay at the Cumberland Hotel by Marble Arch. It was modern, and wonder of wonders, it was reputed to have central heating. It was a splendid billet, and especially so as Hazard's brother-in-law, Hugh Leavell, was also there while he completed his public health assignment with the British. He was soon ferreted out to tell of his narrow escape from death a short while earlier when a bomb went off in the Marble Arch area. It shattered his windows and scattered slivers of glass across his bed. Fortunately, he had been at breakfast.

Jackson's office was in one of the old private homes on Mount Street, while the mess was to be in the basement of the Park Lane. Jackson was away, but his deputy, Brigadier General Telford Taylor, was in charge. Hazard was assigned to him. There was no specific assignment. It was just the general question, "What should Jackson know about Soviet Law?" Hazard set out to work, translated some of the books he had brought along on soviet prosecutors and law, and wrote memoranda. Jackson never did arrive, but Taylor took Hazard to the preparatory conferences. It became clear that the process would take longer than the six weeks that Hazard was to be there. There was a great deal to be done to coordinate the four teams of prosecutors.

The autumn came early, and the Mount Street house was cold, as only unheated English houses can be. Small fires could be burned in some of the grates, but they were only psychologically important. Fortunately, the advisers were an exciting group. Hazard spent a lot of time with the man in the next room, Raphael Lemkin. He was working on the idea that a new crime was to be established in international law, the crime of genocide. The name was his own invention. He was a Polish Jew who felt the need to stop Hitler's kind of slaughter for all time. He was imaginative. Later he became world-famous as the "father" of the Genocide Convention, which was finally sponsored by the United Nations and signed by most of the countries of the world. Lemkin was a dedicated man of great learning. Although quiet to the extreme, his enthusiasm for his task was infectious.

Taylor took Hazard to the meetings with the others. They were a famous and formidable group. The British Attorney General was Sir Hartley Shawcross, who would later become Lord Shawcross, and his Solicitor General was Frank Soskice. The French Prosecutor was DeGaulle's Minister of Justice, M. DeMenthon, while the Soviet Prosecutor was Lt. Gen. Roman Rudenko, later to become the Prosecutor General of the U.S.S.R. Their task was to coordinate four legal systems in one indictment and to devise a coordinated set of procedural law for the trial itself.

It was a comparatist's dream: a chance to make practical use of the knowledge generally reserved for the academic halls. English and American common law are branches on the same tree trunk. French and Soviet law are branches on a separate and distinct tree called the Romanist legal system. It was inspired by the Roman Law, which was reintroduced into Europe by the Inerius school at Bologna in the eleventh century. Russia had inherited from this school through Byzantium in the first instance and by conscious borrowing from Western European models in the nineteenth century as Tsarist Commissions sought to rejuvenate Russian codes.

There were some straightforward problems, such as the gathering of evidence, on which differences in schools of law were of no consequence. Hazard spent much time translating, from the Russian, captions under the photographs of Nazi medical experiments. The pictures were of naked Soviet soldiers and German Jews who had been castrated in an effort to find out the medical consequences. The only problem with the evidence was that it was emerging every day. There were said to be freight cars full of it on sidings in Germany waiting to be opened. It was clear that not all of it could be studied in time for preparation of the indictment. This caused the first conflict between the two legal systems, the common law and the Romanist, since each conceived of an indictment differently.

To the Romanists, both French and Soviet, an indictment must be a complete summation of the evidentiary record. It must notify the accused of the witnesses and documents that will be produced at the trial. To the common lawyer, the indictment need only recite exactly what the charge against him is. He need not be told all the facts, much less the names of the witnesses. He need only know that he is before the court to defend himself against a specific charge of crime. Nothing else may be brought against him during the trial, but there may by any number of surprises at the trial within the confines of the charge.

Here was the nub of the conflict between the teams. The French and Soviets wanted an indictment that included everything, and a preliminary investigation before trial that would explore everything and record it for the Tribunal to use itself. The Romanist trial is only a verification of what the French call the *instruction* and the Russians the *predvaritelnoe sledstvie*. For the common lawyers, there is no *instruction*. There is only the assemblage of information sufficient to convince the prosecutor that he has a good case, and this is traditionally presented to a Grand Jury for verification. The case of the suspects is not reviewed, except insofar as the prosecutor may wish to see if what he has is insufficient. The drama is the trial.

Taylor reported that Jackson wanted drama for the simple reason that he thought that without it the trial would simply "fizzle out" as the public of the world lost interest. Further, he reminded his colleagues that the freight cars of evidence had not been completely explored. There was enough to convince him that there was a case, but he did not want to have to exclude some telling material merely because it was not listed in the indictment. A compromise was reached: The indictment would list some

Drafting the Nuremberg Indictment 85

of the documents and some of the witnesses, but it would not provide the basis for exclusion at the trial of additional witnesses or additional documents that might come to light as the staffs continued to search the freight cars.

Another debate occurred over whether the Nazis could be prosecuted in the alternative. The court would be asked to find the accused guilty on whichever of the alternative counts should be found to be correct. The problem was the charge that a crime against humanity had been committed. Sir Hartley took the position that the acts allegedly constituting war crimes were also crimes against humanity. The war crimes were the atrocities committed on nationals of the prosecuting powers. As to the atrocities committed on German nationals, there was no doubt that they had not up to that time been considered crimes against international law as it then stood. Any hope of punishing the Nazis for what they did to German Jews and Gypsies had to depend upon it being found that there had been a crime against some "higher law" than that in the current books, namely the crime of violating the rules of humanity generally. Shawcross feared, evidently, that the tribunal might find no specific existing rules of law violated by atrocities against English, French, American and Soviet nationals. He wanted to provide the possibility to the Tribunal if it established a "crime against humanity" in connection with atrocities on Germans of finding that the same crime had been committed against the nationals of the prosecuting powers. He hoped that such a crime could be deduced from the general provisions of the Hague Convention.

The French objected to such an alternative plea, for they saw it as a violation of their rule of *non bis in idem* which springs from Roman law, namely that there should be no repetition. The Soviets agreed that their law took the same position, but the Prosecutor said he could accept the British practice in this case. Of course, the Americans were prepared to accept Shawcross's position. The French finally also agreed to provide unity.

The French were not always so cooperative. They permanently split on the issue of the summons to the accused. One of them, Martin Bormann, could not be found anywhere. Rumor had it that he had fled to Argentina. The problem was how to summon him to trial. The Americans suggested a radio broadcast. The British agreed, but the French did not. M. DeMenthon rose in his chair and shouted "Nous avons fait la guerre pour l'affiche." This meant that proper notice of criminal charges was required. There could be no secret charges, and no trials without the accused. The French resistance saw their concept of liberty lodged in proper procedures. DeMenthon wanted a notice to be pasted on the door of the city hall at the last known residence of the accused. To the Americans and British, such service of notice would subject the court to ridicule, for all the world knew that Bormann was wanted: Indeed that was probably why no one could find him. He was in hiding. Finally, it was agreed to post the "affiche" on the door in Berlin, but at the same time to issue and publish by radio the order of the court to appear.

Hazard never got to the trial in Nuremberg. The time needed to prepare the indictment had been much longer than expected. He had to return to Washington to see through the liquidation of the Lend-Lease program for the U.S.S.R. In the midst of a discussion one afternoon, he had to pick up his papers, bid General Taylor goodbye, and rush to the airport. Regrettably, the fog set in for two days, and all he could do was wait for the plane to arrive from the Continent to take him on to New York.

Some days later, he reached Washington, late in the evening. The London experience had been a remarkable one. It put him back into his profession, and prepared him for the post he was to take up in the summer of 1946 at Columbia. But it was not only exciting because of its professional aspects. He had made many friends in London on previous visits, and he enjoyed renewing the relationships. He had a glimpse of the overseas American army as he ate in the officers' mess in the upper diningroom. His simulated rank of Major qualified him for this exalted place. It was still cafeteria style: plastic trays were divided into partitions, into which the mess boys put the blobs of potatoes, vegetables and meat; but the food was a notch above that provided for the captains and lieutenants. The conversation at the table was more mature. Once again he reflected on what turns life could take for a specialist on Soviet Law.

Chapter Eight
THE RUSSIAN INSTITUTE YEARS

THE RUSSIAN INSTITUTE YEARS

The Russian Institute of Columbia University introduced a new structure into education in the United States, the concept of "area studies." Traditionally, universities were structured by department and by professional schools. Cross-disciplinary studies had always been urged as desirable, but few scholars felt themselves to be competent in more than one field of study. Indeed, the idea abroad was that a man or woman who tried to do too many things could not but be shallow. He or she was cursed by being dubbed a "journalist."

Geroid T. Robinson, long-time Professor of Russian History at Columbia University, knew this. When American participation in World War II began, he accepted a call from William Langer, a Harvard historian of long acquaintance, to come to Washington to head a section of the newly created Office of Strategic Services. Its purposes was to explore, as scholars, what might be expected from the Soviet Union as an ally. Robinson was quick to sense that the problem was very real, for Stalin was not prepared to open his country to research, even by an ally intent upon helping it. Stalin's reception of Hopkins and Harriman when the Lend-Lease program was in the making had proved that fact. If the United States was to help the Soviet war effort effectively, it would have to rely on its own research. With this as his aim, Robinson gathered the few American scholars who knew something about one or another discipline as it related to the U.S.S.R. In a sense, it was the first area institute, built upon the work of people like Ruth Benedict. She had attempted to prove in the *Chrysanthemum and the Sword* that the closed Japanese society could be understood by a concerted effort to piece together what scholars knew about it.

As the war moved to its end, Robinson felt that the number of persons who knew about the Soviet Union was too few for a postwar United States that needed to work with the Russians. Robinson never quoted DeToqueville's famous dictum on the Russians and the Americans, but he sensed that the world would become subject to their influence long before it became a commonplace to talk of the "superpowers." He decided to create a program of studies that would prepare considerable numbers of Americans to work in the field, not solely as scholars, but as journalists, businessmen, government officials, diplomats, research staffs for labor unions and international affairs institutes. He gathered around him as consultants persons working in the Soviet field whom he had known for years or come to know in his own office during the war. Among these were Philip E. Mosely, Ernest Simmons,

Abram Bergson, and Hazard. They represented the disciplines of international relations, literature and language, economics, and political science and law. Of course, Robinson added himself as the history component.

The next task was to convince the Columbia University faculty that the concept was valid in a University. Robinson found a colleague at Columbia, in the political science department, who proved a valued strategist in presenting the idea. He was Schuyler C. Wallace, who had conducted for the Navy, during the war, a short course in language and area for officers who were to be assigned abroad. Wallace not only sensed the need for preparing Americans for the postwar world he saw before him, but he also had tried out in practice a method of cross-disciplinary teaching. Robinson and Wallace devised a plan.

Their scheme took into consideration what they knew to be the hostility of men and women in each traditional discipline for the granting of interdisciplinary degrees. Their plan did not call, therefore, for a new Columbia degree. It was to create a coordinating body for interdisciplinary study, not a new department of Russian studies. Each member of this coordinating body would have to meet the scholarly tests of his fellows in the department with which he would be concerned. In short, a political scientist teaching about the Soviet system of government would have to pass the tests for appointment to the political science department, and so on around the circle of departments. An economist of socialist economics would have to be an acceptable economist generally. The coordinating body would bring together scholars within the University concerned with the U.S.S.R. in its various aspects. If a department had no specialist in its field who could qualify also as a knowledgeable person about the U.S.S.R., Robinson would recommend one, and urge his or her appointment. Hopefully, the candidate would pass muster.

With this concept, Robinson and Wallace won the day, and the plan was accepted. Robinson also confided to Hazard that he was not solely interested in his training program for the reasons indicated. He admitted that he had been bored at Columbia before the war working in his narrow field of history; his students had been few, and he wanted to reach more people and expand his own horizon. The Russian Institute met, therefore, his own personal desires.

Having gained the faculty's consent to the new idea, the organizers had to find funds. This they did at the Rockefeller Foundation, where Joseph Willet gave a sympathetic ear to their request for an experimental five-year grant. But this was not all, for the founders had to consider national political sentiment. Although Joseph McCarthy had not yet raised his head, there was suspicion of those who worked in the Russian field. Many people could not forget the mood of the 1920's and 1930's, when Americans who were interested in the new Russia were often presumed to be reds. Robinson and Wallace anticipated that Columbia University would itself be branded as red if it stood alone in the United States with a Russian Institute.

To avoid such a smear, Robinson and Wallace hit upon the idea that they would have to create not only their own Russian Institute, but they would have to stimulate another University to create a competing institute. They turned to Harvard, and to William Langer, who like Robinson had returned to his home campus after completing his wartime service in Washington. Langer agreed to try to set up such a program which he would call a "Russian Research Center." For funds, he turned to John Gardner of the Carnegie Corporation. Gardner showed the same appreciation of the needs of the future, as he did some years later when he created his noted organization, Common Cause. He agreed not only to fund the Harvard program, but to help find talented scholars for its staff. He began telephoning around the country, and even reached Hazard to ask about potential candidates for a role comparable to the one Hazard was to hold at Columbia. In this way, the Harvard Center was born. It would grow to world-wide stature under Langer's leadership, and would pace Columbia for decades as a training ground for specialists. From the Soviet point of view, both became "schools for spies," for their researchers sought to ferret out facts, and it was communist practice to keep as much secret as possible. Soviet suspicions were increased as graduates entered upon their professional lives; many of them became government civil servants not only in the Department of State, the Department of Commerce, the Department of Labor, but also in the intelligence agencies. Others prowled around Eastern Europe as journalists to seek something more than the facts that were made available by the information agencies of the socialist block.

The early applicants for admission to the Russian Institute were numerous and often mature. Many of them had served during the war and had developed a desire to know a great deal about international politics. The Soviet Union was clearly emerging as the primary nation which American policy makers had to deal with. Examples of such students were Marshall Shulman, who came to the fore as Cyrus Vance's specialist on Soviet affairs during the Carter Administration; and Alexander Dallin who became a Director of the Russian Institute for a time after Robinson's retirement, and then moved on to Stanford to achieve fame. There were many more, some of whom climbed the ladder of the diplomatic service to become Ambassador to the U.S.S.R., like

Foy Kohler and Walter Stoessel. Others became Ambassadors to Eastern European socialist countries. A great number continued into scholarly careers as directors of area institutes created on the Columbia model at Illinois, Michigan, and Brown. Many entered area institutes as professors.

Robinson's idea had born fruit just as he had expected it would. When he retired, Philip Mosely took on the Directorship of the program. It had become a heavy responsibility because the nation began to look to the Russian Institute and its Harvard counterpart as sources of information and opinions on the U.S.S.R. Mosely was hounded by the press whenever a striking event occurred in Moscow. He was besieged by refugees from the U.S.S.R. who hoped for introductions to jobs. Finally, it was too heavy a load, and he escaped to the Council on Foreign Relations to become its Director of Studies. The Directorship passed on to Henry Roberts and to Alexander Dallin.

Hazard had sought to avoid all administrative responsibility at Columbia. He made an informal pact with Schuyler Wallace that he would be left free to conduct his own teaching and research, and would be given a minimum of administrative responsibility. He never wanted to be considered a Director. He escaped the task except during one period of crisis when the Director was absent, and he agreed to be Acting Director. The job was unpleasant, for it meant that he had to concern himself with the myriad personal problems of a staff, just as he had done during his five years with Lend-Lease in Washington. He knew that administration was not glorious, although Directors received perquisites of office. They were invited to official functions by the President of the University; they marched in dignified locations in University processions, and they even received an increase in salary. But all of those advantages paled into insignificance because of the pressure to get out an endless series of reports and prepare a budget. One had to listen to a secretary cry dejectedly when there was friction with another employee in the office. And there were the inevitable complaints that someone else had a better desk or a seat nearer a window. There might be those who relish participation in resolving these problems, but Hazard had had his fill in Lend-Lease. He wanted no more of it.

The exciting work of the Russian Institute, from the faculty side, was the development of an educational program. What did an area specialist need to know? All of the professors were agreed that area specialization required cross-cultural experience. Historians would have to study economics, and economists would have to study history. The problem was to determine the mix and the capacity of the student to absorb information during the two years of the program. Wallace had sensed during his wartime program for the Navy that the human being can do more work as a student than is commonly thought possible. He encouraged the Russian Institute professors to require a heavy course load. The program included a major in the student's chosen discipline, and at least one generalized course in each of the other disciplines offered by the Institute program. This in itself was a burden, because the Institute had five professors with five groups of courses, and, in addition, every candidate for a Certificate was required to become proficient in the Russian language.

But that was not all: Every candidate was expected to obtain his degree in addition to a certificate of proficiency in area studies. He or she had to earn an M.A.; a Ph.D. was required to become a teacher. This meant meeting the requirements of the department concerned in the field generally. An historian had to study historiography; an economist, economic theory; a political scientist, methodology, and so on. The burden seemed almost intolerable, and over the years it had to be reduced to require familiarity with fewer area fields. In Hazard's view, the concession to student pressure was perhaps necessitated by humanitarian concerns, of which he was always aware; but from an intellectual point of view, he felt that the Soviet system was a whole that could not be understood without some familiarity with its many components.

Fortunately, for students and faculty alike, the various Universities concerned with Soviet area studies banded together to publish a translation series entitled *Current Digest of the Soviet Press*. It was located at Columbia, and headed by a remarkable scholar-journalist, Leo Gruliow. He had lived in the U.S.S.R. prior to the war; he brought the Russian Institute faculty into his advisory counsel, and he hired people who were being developed in several fields, to be his translators and interpreters. The weekly publication provided a convenience, not only because of its translations, but because of its wide coverage of current events in the U.S.S.R. The reader could follow the theater, music, art, agriculture, industry, communist party policy and practice, state practice, literature, international politics, and all the rest. To this day, the *Current Digest* is invaluable to area studies, and increasingly so, as students are relieved from the obligation to pass examinations in many fields. They can be self-taught, and prove that all learning is not to be achieved through spoon-feeding.

Another publication helped the area specialists and this was also the creation of the Columbia professors. A professional society was created under the name of the American Association for the Advancement of Slavic Studies. Its founders were a small group of professors led by Robinson, Simmons, and Mosely but including experts from other campuses. Because Hazard was a lawyer by profession, he was charged with getting it legally incorporated and on its feet. The Rockefeller Foundation agreed to finance its early years, and Simmons was made managing editor. He had considerable experience, for during the war when the well-established British periodical of the School of Slavonic Studies in the University of London had had to cease publication, it passed the baton to Americans, and Simmons brought out the American Series. With the creation of an Association in the U.S.A. to publish a journal after the British took back their own Slavonic Review, it was logical to begin the U.S. publication.

The dispute over a name for the Association and its Journal is revealing of the fear of red-baiting which existed at the time. At the formation meeting, held at the Harvard Club in New York, Robert Kerner of Berkeley insisted that the name "Russia" be omitted from any titles, and that the word "American" begin any title. He wanted it clear that this was not a front organization to insinuate Soviet propaganda into American scholarship. Consequently, the title of both the Association and the journal began with "American." To avoid "Russia" in the title, the names of both became lengthy, so much so that Hazard's former colleague in his law office questioned whether any organization could endure, without ridicule, a title of AAASS. Some people might get a sense that it was composed of asses.

The journal had an equally long title; the group chose to call it the American Slavic and East European Review. It was obvious that the title of its inspiration, the British Slavonic Review, had some influence, but the East European part of the title had another origin. The colleagues at the Harvard Club argued that there was much in Eastern Europe that was not Slavic, notably the Finns, the Romanians, the Greeks, and the Hungarians. The long title was the result. It lasted throughout Simmons editorship and through the following nine years when Hazard was managing editor. When Donald Treadgold of the University of Washington became the managing editor, the title was simplified to "Slavic Review." To provide continuity, the long old title was preserved in small print on the masthead.

Hazard found the editorship to be both a delight and a chore. The delight was in the constant contact with the scholars who submitted manuscripts and read those of their colleagues prior to publication. He came to know about everyone in the field regardless of discipline. In conjunction with the editorial board, he selected topics for coverage, and invited scholars to write on these topics. It was a small scale operation; there was only one staff member to aid in editing manuscripts, read proofs, and get the journal out. The chore was in financing the journal. The Rockefeller grant had run out in time, and funds had to be found elsewhere. Although the subscription list was long enough to provide a foundation, supplementary income was needed. This meant approaching the various Universities whose professors sat on the editorial board. Everyone pleaded poverty, as has always been the case when a dean is approached. But the editorial board members pressed their deans, and small sums were obtained.

Further, the AAASS was expanded. With the graduation of increasing numbers of specialists, there was a larger pool on which to draw. Memberships were doubled, tripled, and quadrupled until the Association became a full-fledged professional association. It now numbers members in the thousands, holds a national meeting annually, and has regional branches who hold meetings from time to time. *The Slavic Review* is its creature, as it always has been, but it has taken to itself the *Current Digest of the Soviet Press*, a bibliographical volume of studies in the field, and special volumes of materials collected from the *Current Digest*, as with all of the documents relevant to a communist party congress. At its annual meetings it honors a senior scholar in the area field with a citation and a banquet. Hazard, as one of the last surviving founders, was so honored in 1978. The citation was read by Marshall Shulman, who had been a student in his first class of 1946, and who at the time ranked as "Ambassador," because of his role as adviser on Soviet affairs in the Department of State.

Publications have always been an aim of the Russian Institute. Its professors were urged to publish and given research grants to assist them. Hazard, like the others, was a beneficiary of such a grant. Out of it came his first book after his dissertation which had been completed at the University of Chicago under the guidance of Samuel N. Harper, Professor of Russian History and Max Rheinstein, Professor of Comparative Law. One would have called the second book a *habilitation*, had it been in Germany, but in the United States it was but an item in a bibliography. In a sense the book was a reassurance to Columbia that it had not made a mistake in granting tenure to a thirty-eight-year-old newcomer who had had no period of apprenticeship.

Perhaps a word on that appointment is in order at this point. Ordinarily, teachers began their career at the bottom of the ladder, as instructors, and worked their way up. Hazard began at the top as a full professor. His mother-in-law never really accepted the idea that he had made such an exalted start; her lifetime had been spent in the company of Harvard professors, and she knew the long route to the top. Still, the evidence was there. Hazard's title was, from the start, "Professor of Public Law." Wallace had asked him what title he would like to have and he chose the one that was given. The reason was simple: He was a lawyer, and the title conveyed that idea; and the department he was to enter was the Department of Public Law and Government. In his new role he was to teach courses on both Soviet law and Soviet political institutions. At that time, political scientists were not as hostile to law-trained people as they were to become later. Although Hazard's doctoral degree from Chicago was a J.S.D., rather than a Ph.D. in political science, Columbia University was prepared to accept him, and so were his political science colleagues. Today, it would be otherwise, for political science departments now insist that appointees have a Ph.D. Fortunately for Hazard, the wheel had not turned that far in 1946.

What made the tenure possible was Columbia's pressing need for someone to teach political science courses on the U.S.S.R., and the fact that persons in the field were scarce. Hazard's hand was tipped by an additional fact. The University of Chicago was also interested in appointing Hazard. An interview was arranged, and Hazard flew there, accompanied by his wife, Susan. Hazard knew the Chicago group well, and even its President, Robert Maynard Hutchins. He had been a professor at Yale, and later the President of Chicago University, during Hazard's student days. He had a jaunty, even sassy, way of speaking about serious things. He offered Hazard a post as Associate Professor at a salary higher than Columbia was offering but without tenure. The position looked attractive, but it would have been a post without the backing of an area institute, and it would have lacked the security tenure provided.

Hazard chose Columbia for the reasons implied in his doubts about Chicago. He thought that the environment of an area institute would broaden his horizons, and make him a more complete scholar. He also thought that a time might come when political pressures from red baiters would become heavy enough to threaten his tenure. Although Chicago could be assumed to be a step above such considerations, history was replete with appointments that had fizzled out for political reasons; and there was no reason to take a chance when another offer was before him. So Columbia was chosen over Chicago. Years later, Chicago tried again, after the death of Karl Llewellyn. Edward Levi, the man who had shared the office next to Hazard's in the Law Library when Hazard was completing his dissertation in 1938-39, called to invite Hazard to take his place. (Levi later became the Attorney General of the United States under President Ford.) Levi said that Hazard was not quite as odd a scholar as Llewellyn, but he had some of the same characteristics, and the faculty liked him. Again, Hazard decided for Columbia, where he had become very much at home, and where the Russian Institute environment had proved to be not only congenial but stimulating. The same decision was made on other occasions. The University of Michigan offered the chair of comparative law vacated by its long-time professor, Hessel E. Yntema; and on two occasions, Stanford asked Hazard to come to create a Russian Institute. The Stanford offer sounded exceptionally attractive because the place had been found enjoyable during two summer school sessions spent there. But the thought of having to find the funds for such an Institute was too much to contemplate. Hazard had disliked administration; he had reached an agreement with Wallace at Columbia that he need not undertake it; and there was no reason to retreat from that position.

To return to the second book: It was to grow out of a series of articles begun in 1936 when the *Harvard Law Review* had written Hazard in Moscow to ask for an article on Soviet Law. Hazard had accepted, although he was very busy trying to keep abreast of his studies at the Moscow Juridical Institute. He had completed only the first year of his studies, but he put together his notes on courses for that first year and embellished them with references to much of the Soviet literature. The article was completed in early 1936 and sent to Cambridge, but soon a reply was received from the editor that the *Review* dared not publish an article on Soviet law without a balancing one on fascist law. The editor explained that the *Columbia Law Review* had received such a balancing article from Henry Steiner of U.C.L.A., and both editors wanted to print them both in one issue. Hazard agreed, and the first article, "Soviet Law: An Introduction," appeared in the *Columbia Law Review* in December 1936. It headed the bibliography which was to grow over the years, and perhaps had some influence emotionally on Hazard when he chose Columbia over Chicago as a home in 1946.

During the wartime years at Lend-Lease, Hazard kept his franchise by working on weekends in his small study. He kept the door closed against his growing family of children, and produced a series of studies. He also taught, during the lunch hour, a course in Soviet foreign policy at what was then called the School of Advanced International Studies, later incorporated in Johns Hopkins University. With this growing list of publications, he entered Columbia. His research grant permitted him to retain the services of a former Polish prosecutor who knew Russian, one George Krynsky. Krynsky was given the task of culling the unindexed Soviet legal periodicals for judicial decisions. At the time, the writings on Soviet law were based, in European fashion, primarily on theoretical texts and magisterial articles. No one was studying the Soviet cases. Hazard was determined to do so because he felt as a common lawyer that no general statement could be believed unless it was supported by a case. He also liked the sociological facts revealed in the judicial opinions.

Krynsky made this type of painstaking culling possible, and his cards, with the essence of the decisions in Russian, opened the way for the 1953 book.

Publication did not take place until 1953 because the burden of teaching in those years at Columbia was too heavy to permit concentration on a book. The first opportunity to sit down to think out a pattern for such a volume came during the first sabbatical, which Hazard spent as Fulbright Visiting Professor of Law at the University of Cambridge. The invitation had come as a result, as so often happened in earlier years, of unexpected circumstances, on two occasions. The first was the fact that the noted French professor of Comparative Law at the University of Paris, René David, who was interested in Soviet law, had read some of Hazard's articles. When UNESCO asked him to suggest names of scholars from around the world to attend a conference designed to form a new International Committee for Comparative Law, he had suggested Hazard so as to meet him. When they met in the UNESCO headquarters in Paris in 1948, they became immediate friends. David had himself studied at Cambridge and had invited his old colleague C.J. Hamson to the conference as well. Hamson was noted as a specialist on the French Conseil d'Etat. He and Hazard also struck it off immediately, and when he went home, he began to organize a visiting professorship which came to a head in 1952. Hazard was invited, and asked to give a course on Soviet law.

He took with him to England reprints of his articles, plus the Krynsky notes on over 150 Soviet law cases. In the very cold environment of a Cambridge house, but with the stimulation of having to give weekly lectures, he sat down and completed a volume. It was recommended to editors at the University of London, who chose to put it in their series of volumes. So in 1953, after Hazard's return to Columbia, it appeared as *Law and Social Change in the U.S.S.R.* David came into the picture again, for it caught his eye, and he asked for permission to translate and publish it in France. He suggested that since it was so heavily oriented toward the common law approach, it would require an introduction to Romanist oriented scholars. Hazard was delighted at the opportunity to move into francophonic circles, and he agreed to wait until David had done what seemed necessary.

The wait seemed interminable, but at last word came from David that the translation was finished; but the preface had seemed inadequate. He had decided that a whole volume was necessary to expose the theory and history of Soviet law, without which a Continental lawyer would think that the book was incomplete. Consequently, there were now two books instead of one, and they would be published as David *et* Hazard, *Le Droit*

Soviétique. They appeared under the imprint of one of the noted Rue Soufflot publishers in 1954. Then the Spanish dean of the International Faculty for Comparative Law, in which Hazard was later to give regular summer lectures, picked up the volumes and had them put into Spanish and published in Buenos Aires. Thus the word was spread after its humble beginnings with a Russian Institute research grant.

The David *et* Hazard volume had unexpected repercussions some years later when Hazard and his wife Susan were sitting at a dinner table with the eminent Konrad Zweigert. He was formerly a judge of the German Constitutional Court, and Director of the Max Planck Institute for International Private Law at the University of Hamburg. To make polite conversation, Zweigert asked Hazard what he did. After his reply that he worked in Soviet law, Zweigert showed his familiarity in the field by saying, "Connaissez-vous le livre par David et quelqu'un d'autre?" Hazard replied, perhaps too impishly, that "Je suis le quelqu'un d'autre." Zweigert's handsome, ruddy face turned even redder, but he kept his composure. The two became good friends.

Subsequent experience with the writing of books suggested that it took a sabbatical to put each one into shape. A third book was begun with a released time grant from the Russian Institute, under which the teaching load was reduced, with the Institute taking over from the University's general budget, a part of a professor's salary. The result of this grant was the volume that was to be published in 1960, *Settling Disputes in Soviet Society*. This book utilized the vast Heinrich Freund library of Soviet law which the owner had collected during the years from 1917 to 1933 while a professor in Breslau, not far from the Soviet frontiers. The collection is still recognized as one of the major Soviet law libraries in the Western world. Hazard bought it from Freund's widow to augment his own library, which had begun to grow in 1934 when Hazard went to Moscow. Together they provided an unparallelled record for a history of the formative years of Soviet law. Today the library has been placed in the rare document section of the Columbia University Library, and most of it has been filmed on microfiche by the International Documentation Company of Zug, Switzerland, to be available to the world.

In 1954 when Hazard began to put the 1960 book together, the Freund library was untouched. Its materials included not only the earliest publications of 1917 and 1918 but typewritten circulars of the People's Commisariat of Justice. Hazard set up a table in a room of his house and methodically went through the materials. On his next sabbatical at the University of Geneva in 1959, Hazard organized and polished the materials into manuscript form. The volume became a history of the years 1917 to 1925 in the formulation of a legal system following the Bolsheviks' arrival in power with a nihilistic approach to law. In a way, it could be seen as proof that even those who detest a formal legal system cannot do without it. The book was very successful, and when all copies were sold out, Columbia University Press had it reprinted in 1978 by Octagon.

Summers also were given over to long hours of typing. One of the most successful of these summers was the one in 1955 when Hazard decided to accept the invitation of an editor of a comparative politics series to be published by the University of Chicago Press. Hazard was asked to write a textbook on the *Soviet System of Government* for the series. The manuscript grew quickly, since Hazard had his classnotes and had read widely the burgeoning literature in this field. When the manuscript reached the editors, the readers had mixed opinions. Two were enthusiastic; one said he would not give the book to a single student. Of course, this was depressing, but the Chicago editors decided to take the chance. Time has justified their decision. The book has been updated and in 1980 a fifth edition was published. The book sold over 100,000 copies, with an edition published in India, and Swedish, and Korean translations. It was a synthesis of many people's work rather than a work of original scholarship, but it seems to have met a teaching need.

Other sabbaticals or research leaves offered similar opportunities for Hazard to write. One was spent in 1961-62 at the Institute for Advanced Study of the Behavioral Sciences in Palo Alto. That fascinating year opened new vistas as Hazard began to write the first casebook for the teaching of Soviet law. It was his view that a Romanist-type legal system could be taught with a casebook, and Oceana Publications, Inc. published it. Its three editions have proved that it served a purpose.

The most romantically different year was in 1966 when the Hazards took a trip around the world, beginning in Guinea and Mali to observe the workings of socialism. The idea had developed in 1964 when Hazard held a Ford Foundation grant to do research at the University of Dakar for six weeks on African socialism. A paper on négritude was the result, and Hazard longed for a look at two Senegalese neighbors who claimed to be more authentically socialist. After Africa, Hazard went to Egypt for a glimpse of Arabian socialism, and then he and his wife spent six weeks in Teheran, where he gave daily lectures on Soviet law. French was the medium because the interpreter only knew French and the noted Professor Hassan Afchar, who had arranged the series, only knew French and wanted to be able to make interpretive comments as the lectures progressed. The Shah was then engaged in developing what he called the "white revolution," and the Hazards were taken each weekend on excursions from one end of the country to another to see what was being done. At the time it seemed that the modernization program parallelled that of the Soviets to the north but without the terror and the suffering the latter brought in its wake.

From Teheran the couple moved through India to the Far East and finally reached Hawaii and began the second term of the academic year at the East West Center. In the spring of 1967 Hazard began writing his major comparative study of law in the communist world. For such an effort, a team of experts and considerable funding had been required. Jerome A. Cohen of Harvard, with whom Hazard had given a pioneering seminar on comparative communist law at Berkeley in 1961-62, had joined in the request to the Ford Foundation for a large grant. They were successful, and Hazard was immediately able to retain Alexander W. Rudzinski, a noted Polish jurist with experience on the Polish delegation to the United Nations; and Lin Fu-shun, a Taiwanese scholar, and now Professor of Law in the National Taiwan University.

The team worked for some years preparing memoranda on the approach to law by various communist states and taught a seminar on the topic at the Columbia Law School. It was this mass of material that Hazard took to Hawaii to put into his typewriter as he looked out over Manoa valley toward the sea. Upon completion, the manuscript was sent to the University of Chicago Press, and was accepted and published in 1969 under the title: *Communists and their Law: a Search for the Common Core of the Legal System of the Marxian Socialist States.* Hazard felt exhausted and doubted that he would ever again undertake such a lengthy project.

Throughout the term at Hawaii, other senior fellows at the Center conducted a seminar on development, which caught Hazard's imagination because of his work in Africa. He attended and the seminar became the seed which led him, upon his return to Columbia, to introduce a seminar on "Socialist models for development." Its members were graduate students from Africa, Asia and the Caribbean. Many returned to their homelands to fill positions in government and universities. In a sense, Hazard found new stimulus to occupy his time especially in his fifties. That apparently is an age when scholars tend to tire unless they find interesting projects to occupy their time.

Socialism, as a model for development and its impact upon law, became one of the strings to Hazard's bow. Pursuit of this new hobby took him to Algeria one summer at the invitation of the Minister of Justice to observe what was happening to law under this new stimulus, and to Guyana another summer where he was guided by the Attorney

General in the application of socialist ideas to a legal system founded on common law rather than Romanist law.

Hazard continued to teach at the Russian Institute even after his formal retirement in 1977. By that time Hazard had been placed in the chair of the Nash Professor of Law, and his emeritus title bore that name. He was invited to continue to teach his courses under Columbia's general policy that utilized retired professors as long as they wished to teach and could attract students.

Hazard agreed to continue because he liked to teach and wanted to keep the Russian Institute's program as full as possible. Few other teachers in the United States had developed an interest in Soviet public administration, and the course continued to attract students. In the law school, W. Randle Edwards assumed responsibility for the seminar on law in the communist world. His specialty was China, and he invited Hazard to continue with him to discuss the U.S.S.R. and the socialist systems of Africa.

The Russian Institute continued to prosper, and attracted students in steady numbers, although not as many as in the first years. The staff of professors had expanded as new disciplines were added to the original five. Sociology, geography, art, and a wide variety of literature courses concerning nineteenth century Russia and the Soviet period were included. Robinson's dream had proved its worth.

Chapter Nine
THE CHURCH AND ITS PEOPLE

THE CHURCH AND ITS PEOPLE

Churchgoing was routine for Hazard's Episcopalian Mother. The family rented a pew at St. Paul's Church in Syracuse. For as long as they could remember, little John and Gibson were dressed in their olive colored velvet suits with Eton collars each Sunday and taken along to services. They sat under the eye of Dr. Hadley as he preached from the pulpit, and they never even squirmed. It just was not done.

As they grew a bit older, they were entered into the Sunday school program, and walked down James Street alone to attend the school, which occurred before church. It was a frightening walk at times, because the drunken Irishmen of the town, who were the derelicts, roamed the empty streets early Sunday mornings, after a night in the bars. Every orderly family became prohibitionist, and Hazard remembered hearing woeful tales of the Irish mothers who waited at the factory gates to get the pay envelope before their husbands ran off to the bars. Sunday mornings were living proof of the evils of alcoholism and the rock on which "Volsteadism" rested. It was this upsurge of sentiment that led finally to enactment of the amendment to the United States Constitution that prohibited the sale of liquor. On the walk down James Street, nearly every house had a large sign in its front window reading simply "DRY," and it gave strength to the feeling that something would be done, the more so since on occasion the toughs would sweep in from outside to throw rocks at the windows to give substance to the liquor war.

With such a start among the churchgoers, Hazard never went through the soul searching of those who had to be converted later in life. Churchgoing was just the same as school going. It was a routine. Dr. Hadley used to say that when the little boy grew up he would be a crucifer. Perhaps he would have been had his father lived, but with Ada's decision to send her boy away to preparatory school at the age of twelve the time never arrived to carry the cross.

At The Hill, it was easy to continue the routine. It was a school famous for its religious atmosphere. Mrs. John Meigs, the widow of the founder, lived on to interest the boys in missionary work. She conducted a Sunday morning group that studied the mission fields and the Bible. Each spring they went on a picnic with milk cans full of lemonade and pans of gooey cinnamon buns. Religion could be fun in her lexicon. She had been very successful over the years, and famous preachers of the day whom she had persuaded to enter the field would come from time to time to preach at Sunday chapel.

Hazard fell right into the routine. He played his violin in the chapel orchestra so he was up front anyway, but he also was active in what was called the YMCA. This was a Thursday night activity when visiting laymen with a religious bent came to enthrall the boys with stories about the interesting social work they were doing. It had some part to play in assuring that there would be boys attending the "mission" on Chicken Hill behind the school which ministered to the Pennsylvania Dutch workers of the neighborhood. Hazard used to pump the organ for the hymns and still remembers watching the wind gauge on the rear above the long handle attached to the bellows. When the red liquid dropped below the indicated danger spot, he would lean into the work and drive it up again.

Routines continued at Yale. The chapel was no longer compulsory, but its chaplain, Elmore McKee, saw to it that boys with a background like Hazard's were brought quickly into the life of the religious group. He linked the chapel to the YMCA which was called Dwight Hall. This group had its own secretary who organized weekend retreats at various spots and saw to the running of the Yale Hope Mission. The latter institution was an eye-opener, for it was outside of Hazard's prior experience. The Chicken Hill Mission at The Hill ministered to solid, orderly, but simple folk. The Yale counterpart was for the derelicts, the very people Hazard had dodged on his way down James Street to Sunday school as a child. Its message was that something could be done for them, and that was encouraging.

Hazard went on to its board of student advisers. Its direction was in the hands of a hard bitten old Scot and his wife, both of whom had been saved from a life of liquor. They knew the problems and they knew the cure. They gathered around them others who had been saved. The mission had a cafeteria and beds in a dormitory. It helped get odd jobs for those who wanted to start on the road back. The one obligation that the men had to observe was to attend chapel services where lively gospel hymns were sung and where those who had been saved gave their testimonials. With hindsight it is possible to say that it was what had been called by cynics the gospel of "rice Christians," one got fed if one participated. That may be so, but it did provide a place which put some hope into the future of the derelicts. It sold tickets to the meals to the well-to-do of Prospect Street, and these were available to distribute to panhandlers as the purchasers strolled across the New Haven Green.

The weekend retreats were stretched at times to include a winter vacation week on the campus of the Mt. Herman school in Massachusetts. It was there that the boys met girls from similar programs in the girls schools. There were hayrides on sleighs pulled across the squeaking snow, and marshmallow roasts around the fire, and, of course, there were discussions of social problems. Philip Randolph who created the Pullman Porters Union was often present to talk about the problems of the blacks, and of unionism. Sherwood Eddy came to excite the students about the gospel. It was old-fashioned revivalism, not as simple as that of Billy Sunday who was leading converts down the sawdust trail in the big auditoria of the great cities, but an approach which lost its appeal among college students in the decades to follow.

In law school there was the Harvard Chapel to which fewer students went than had been the case at Yale, but Hazard still found friends who wanted to attend. He was beginning to take a new kind of interest in the church, one not so much based on routines but on thinking about its values. By law school, Hazard had been around the world. He had seen the world's great religions. In a sense he had had a practical course in comparative religion. He had noted the mysticism, the extraordinarily different practices, from those who found salvation from bathing in the Ganges, to those who called back the spirits by clapping their hands in Japan before the Shinto shrines. He began to see his own Christian liturgy as a sort of mumbo jumbo developed over ages by the church to attract the attention of the peasants of Europe. Coming forward with incense and candles to read the gospel in the center aisle was a practice which had its historical origins. It demonstrated to the peasants that something extraordinary was to happen, namely the reading of the gospel, the word of Jesus Christ himself.

Liturgy could be beautiful, and beauty had its place, but it was only an historical relic. What really mattered must be something else. Hazard began to search for what it was that kept him going to church. Perhaps it was the beauty of the music, for he was deeply moved by his long career in music. Perhaps it was the architecture of the great churches, but he had spent much time in little ones as well as he wandered about. Finally, it began to dawn on him that churchgoing was satisfying because it put him among people who tried in varying degrees to put aside the greed, the cruelty, the shortsightedness that was everywhere in life. In short, it was a haven for the good people, not in any silly sense of the word, but in the sense of those trying to eliminate from their own lives the evil aspects of social relationships. They would get encouragement from associating with each other on Sunday mornings and in doing the work of the church in the community.

This was not to say that Hazard did not see how some persons exploited their churchgoing. He remembered a talk given by the then president of the American Bar Association who told the Harvard law students that churchgoing attracted clients, and he recommended it to each of them to help improve their income. This meant that there were careerists among those in the pews, but realization of that fact was not allowed to overshadow the sense that there were people present for what seemed to Hazard the laudable reasons.

When the children came along following his marriage to the daughter and granddaughter of an Episcopalian bishop, church attendance was, of course, part of the Sunday routine. St. John's in Washington was the starting point, and church continued to be an influence at St. George's when they returned to New York. The hustling of children through breakfast to pile them into the stationwagon for the ride downtown was a Sunday morning chore. They seemed to have less affection for Sunday school than Hazard remembered of his own childhood.

Hazard found himself being drawn increasingly into the administration of St. George's, first as an usher, and then as a vestryman. St. George's was noted as a liberal and low church. It had no candles, no incense, indeed no cross and no crucifer at the time. One could not criticize the liturgy in its simplicity as being mumbo jumbo. Its vitality was in the spirit of comradeship among its parishioners and in the vibrant leadership of Rector Edward O. Miller. He was young, musical, full of good humor, and an activist. St. George's seemingly had everything Hazard wanted. His wife, Susan, took up her work on the altar guild and in myriad parish activities for which she had, in a sense, been trained as a girl in a clergyman's family.

The vestry was composed of very prominent people, and its senior warden, C.C. Burlingham, had been a force in the cleaning up of New York following scandals in the 1930's. It was a church concerned with the city, and with its problems. The Rector's sermons were directed toward those problems, and they were for the educated people who made up a large part of the congregation.

At the same time, up at Columbia University Chaplain John Krumm conducted Bible classes for the professors. His emphasis was upon the history of the church and of the Bible. It particularly appealed to those who did not find their interest in liturgy, but who wanted something that would fit into their lives of research. In short, they were what Adlai Stevenson later called eggheads, and they wanted a faith for eggheads. Krumm gave them that, and all went well until he was called away to become a bishop. Then James Pike was brought in. He was different.

Pike adored liturgy. He dressed in costumes from ancient English tradition. He was a converted Roman Catholic, and the pomp of the Roman Catholicism remained in his soul. He did not excite the same respect among the eggheads as had Krumm, although he was respected;

he had vigor, he had been a lawyer, he had an intellect, and he could organize campus events. Finally, he went on to the Cathedral of St. John the Divine to become its dean, where he arranged for ever-more-glorious liturgies, and then was elected bishop of Northern California.

But then trouble began at St. George's. The rector had an operation for ileitis, which took out a large part of his intestines. It seemed to affect his character. He became a dictator, unable to be thwarted in any plan. He dissolved the parish council; he broke up the two clubhouses in which the church provided homes for young people just arrived in New York for their first jobs; he dissolved various parish committees, and, finally, he started on the vestry because it would not agree to his policies. The church had been left a large endowment by J. Pierrepont Morgan in the early years of the century, from which it had financed deficits from time to time. Now, the deficits were large, as contributions fell off, partly because disaffected parishioners were leaving.

Miller's argument was attractive to some parishioners: An endowed church would do better to use its endowment to help the community and finally close its doors when the money was gone than adopt a policy of survival. The vestry, being composed of prominent bankers, businessmen, lawyers and academics took the view that a church ought to live on a budget that would be balanced most of the time. The vestrymen thought the church would not lose contributors if the Rector did not antagonize some of the wealthy givers. They decided that he had to go, but this suggestion enraged him. Finally, it was Hazard's role by chance that started the ball rolling. The Rector was constantly spending over the budget and then presenting the bills to the vestry for approval. Finally, when he decided to place pink carpets in the aisles of the church over the old Dutch tiles which had been its pride, Hazard said he thought carpets would make it look like a funeral parlor. The Rector stomped out of the meeting, only to return when coaxed by one of the elderly women vestrypersons.

The vestry decided to go to the Bishop. He received them, but indicated that he did not want trouble in the parish. He had sensed that the Rector would take the issue to the papers, and the Bishop was not a man to want publicity of an unhappy parish. The vestry decided there was nothing to do but resign, and this they did *en masse*. Of course, it had no effect. The Rector found people who supported him, and indeed, he was a charmer for all except those who had to meet with him on parish policy. He put through an election of his own team. But that was not the end.

The new vestry experienced the same problems when they were in the seats of those responsible by law for the finances of the parish. They, too, decided to go to the Bishop. By this time bishops had changed. The new man, Paul Moore, who was not a timid man, arranged a contract of departure under which the Rector would retire with a financial settlement. The church, in its nearly bankrupt state, would unite with two other churches in the same region of New York under the rector of one of these other churches, and the day was saved. Slowly, St. George's in its new role as a church of a combined parish recovered, but the way was rough.

From Hazard's point of view, it was a lesson in problems arising with men of the cloth. They were just as human as anyone else, although parishioners are inclined to place them on a pedestal and to entrust them with everything. The St. George's conflict showed that the institution of the church is peopled with some who do not accept the role of the saintly man, who is prepared to work out problems with those around him. To be sure there were those who believed that Jesus was also a man of determination and drove his disciples to do what he wanted. There was no record in the Bible of established democratic procedures to determine policy. Hazard came to believe that clergymen of the day were not divine, and they could not support dictatorial policies with defenses based upon the life of Christ. In America, at least, the church must be run as a democratic institution, as prescribed and enforced by the state under the religious law in each of the states. And, further, clergymen proved themselves as adept as politicians as they masked issues, controlled votes, and even concealed what they were doing so that only when it was hard to reverse the process did the action appear to the parish for what it was: the destruction of the parish.

In spite of these experiences, Hazard continued to attend church wherever he was. He liked the company churches provided, and when he traveled in foreign lands, he found the local churches provided a view of the life of the community. As the Anglican-Episcopalians are in many places, their parishes provide a home away from home. When they do not exist, there is often a Church of Christ which is interdenominational, and if there is neither, there is usually a Roman Catholic Church where the mass, at least, is familiar because Bishop Cranmer copied it when he wrote the prayer book centuries ago that provided the liturgy for his Anglicans.

Hazard has been among those Episcopalians who opposed dictation from the National Church through its Convention. He has argued that each parish should be permitted to choose its prayer book, the Cranmer book, or the revised prayer book which is said to be more inspirational to the current generation of young people. He would let each parish conduct its own financial affairs, unless it is driven in the direction of bankruptcy by a rector who will not keep within budgets. At that point, a fatherly bishop can be a final court of appeal. And, of course, he would never countenance a system where the church, and other religious institutions, are financed by the state as in Europe and many other places. He shares the founding fathers' distrust of a link between church and state, although he sees the need for the state prosecutor when a prelate embezzles funds. That type of criminal penalty is not for the church to enforce through ecclesiastical courts. Churches, like all other institutions within society, must be held to the common standards for society generally when the management of property is concerned. Churches are not above the common law of crime.

After the merger of St. George's with Calvary and Holy Communion, Susan was elected to the vestry and became its clerk. She was placed on the committee on property, which gave her a chance to participate in decisions relating to the large number of buildings which the parish now owned. She was in the middle of things, so Hazard kept up his interest through her. Regrettably, she had to leave the vestry when the various visiting professorships during the emeritus period began, but on returns to New York, the Hazards were as active as they could be in helping with the minor chores on 16th Street.

Hazard's early childhood experiences with religion and the church, naturally influenced his attitudes and opinions toward communists with their beliefs in atheism. He would not, of course, have denied them their right to be atheists, because he was a liberal when it came to matters of conscience, but he resented their effort to destory the church in the new Russia. On his first brief visit in 1930 he and his colleagues had attended mass in the great Cathedral of the Savior on the hill overlooking the Moscow River. The young men, who understood little of the liturgy, had been greatly moved by the choral singing that included singers from the state opera company. Despite their lack of understanding of the mysticism of the Orthodox church, the quartet of travelers were impressed by the evident reverence of the parishioners as they lighted their candles, kissed the ikons and raised their voices in the chants. To musically-oriented Hazard the swelling chords coming from the throats of hundreds of singers in a great nave contributed to an inexplicable sense of emotion.

Upon Hazard's return to Moscow in 1934, he found that the cathedral had been raised to the ground ostensibly to make room for a palace of Soviets projected to be the tallest building in the world. The fact that it was never built suggested that it was not city planning that had brought the end of the Cathedral but a desire to remove the principal symbol of religion in the nation's capital. Other churches were closed and the buildings allowed to fall into ruin. Government policy had not yet advanced to see them as architectural monuments to Russia's glorious past. The few churches still open were sparsely attended, and it was official policy to discriminate against those who manifested their faith by church attendance.

Of course, no obvious believer could become a member of the Communist Party, therefore high political office was denied to churchgoers. Further, the constitution, although it granted freedom of conscience to citizens, denied them the right to propagate their faith. Believers could only attend mass. They could not conduct Sunday school. Only the atheists through the Society of the Godless could preach their convictions to the multitude, usually through converted churches that were anti-religious museums that exposed the fraud and corruption of the church and the scientific proof that man came not from God but from multiplication of cells.

Hazard began to wonder whether the communism of Stalin had not abandoned the humanism preached by Marx along with his atheism. With the campaign to discredit the church, the government left no institution of humanistic orientation to serve as the conscience of the regime. There was no brake left to restrain the arbitrary use of power by the Kremlin's inner circle. Hazard was not alone in sensing this vacuum. He found later, when he studied Algerian socialism, that Algeria's leaders had sensed the same thing. When they adopted socialism as their creed, their scholars wrote that Islam had to be preserved as a humanizing influence. They would not follow the Stalinist model's attitude toward religion.

Likewise, when Hazard served as a visiting professor in Senegal, he found that the Chief Justice was writing that Islam was socialist and not incompatible with a socialist political faith. Africans were sensing that socialism could be brutal if devoid of the humanism of religion. Indeed, they wrote that there could be a healthy interplay between socialism and Islam: Socialism would be humanized, and Islam would be cleansed of the excrescences of the centuries which had no place in modern societies. Modern Islamic socialists wanted reform of the Mosque, not its abolition. The Algerians wrote into their constitution that the state was both socialistic and Islamic. Even the socialists of Sri Lanka sensed the same need, for their constitution was to declare Sri Lanka both socialist and Buddhist.

To be sure the Russian Orthodox Patriarch had proved himself to be a thorn in Stalin's side in the 1920's, and priests opposed to the policy of collectivization of agriculture in the early 1930's had been ousted from their parishes and sometimes imprisoned. It is possible that had there been no destruction of churches, no persecution of priests, no militant atheists to interfere with church ceremonies, the church would have dropped its opposition earlier than it did and made its peace with the regime as it had done over the centuries with the Tsars. The final reconciliation had to await Stalin's move under the threat of defeat by the Nazis in the Second World War. He then permitted the church to elect a Patriarch and to reopen its seminary for priests.

While the constitution had never been amended to authorize propagation of religion in Sunday school, and while legislation still hampered congregations with requirements that they obtain licenses to function, and while the faithful could not look forward to advancement in the political hierarchy, there emerged in the 1980's an uneasy, but observable, toleration of those whose faith required them to associate with others in the mass—at least for the Orthodox. Traditional opposition to what the Tsar had looked upon as heretical sects continued, but, at least, among the Orthodox Christians the severe pressures of the 1920's and 1930's had abated.

To Hazard the relaxation of pressure on the church marked an improvement in the way in which the regime ran the government. However, he continued to deplore the hostility still manifested toward congregations other than those of the Orthodox church, especially toward those of the dissenting Christian sects and of the Jewish community.

The U.S.S.R. had become so strong by the 1960's after Stalin's death in 1953, and so many steps had been taken to moderate the rigor of his regime that the dogged adherence to militant atheism as official policy seemed to be an unnecessary relic of the revolution. In private conversation, some of Moscow's lawyers with whom Hazard associated admitted that their leaders no longer needed to oppose religion for security reasons and that enemies of the regime were made unnecessarily both at home and abroad by continuation of anti-religious policies. Still, these perceptive critics of policy seem to have had no influence. Militant atheism remained a pillar of Soviet policy, and perseverance in this policy seemed irrational and misguided. For Hazard, the Soviet system would do well to abandon it.

Chapter Ten
EMERITUS AND ALL THAT

EMERITUS AND ALL THAT

"Congratulations, John." Never were words more unwelcome. They were spoken by William McGill, President of Columbia University, as he stood on the sidewalk in front of the Law School. He had his hand out and greeted Hazard who took it unhappily. He knew that McGill was referring to the fact that the University trustees had just voted emeritus status to Hazard as he ended his 68th year. Under University rules, the status need not be conferred upon retirement, but Hazard knew of only one case when it had been withheld. Generally, it was the parting gesture at the end of a teaching career. It meant that the teacher, although usually invited back to give courses for a few more terms, was on the shelf. Worse yet, an emeritus professor lost prestige and public esteem. His letters of recommendation of students for jobs, his voice at meetings, and his manuscripts, were all somehow greeted with respect but were considered lacking when compared to the opinions and work of an active person.

From the personal work-load point of view, the emeritus status had advantages. The retired professor no longer had to sit on committees. He could do what he wanted, rather than what the dean wanted. But these burdens had never been too heavy for Hazard, even though his duties had been doubled with seats in both the Political Science and Law Faculties. The deans had respected his wish to be free of administrative work. He had once served as acting director of the Russian Institute to help out the director who wanted to take a leave, but he had refused the task on two other occasions; one of them was at the very moment of his retirement. Generally, he had been free to offer the courses he wanted to give, write the books he wanted to write, and to take leaves when they fitted into his plans.

In the United States, one's level of prestige seemed to decline after formal retirement. Foreign universities knew that they could invite the emeritus professor to teach on their campuses with some expectation that the invitation would be accepted. So it was with Hazard. Sydney was the first University to step into the gap. Hazard had often used his sabbaticals to visit abroad. He had been to England, Geneva, and Iran for terms during his active career, and had taught summer terms in Tokyo, France and in a variety of countries with the International Faculty of Comparative Law, which was peripatetic. He and his wife enjoyed the visits, and while the children were young, they went along, too.

The Sydney professorship was a new experience. It was in an

unknown region of the world, "down under," with reversed seasons. The new Professor of Jurisprudence, who had been appointed to replace the retired Julius Stone, had an interest in Soviet law. Being both Singapore Chinese and a London barrister, she knew both the Chinese language and the common law. She specialized in the impact of socialism on the Chinese legal system under Mao Tse-tung. This had brought her to Columbia some years earlier, where she and Hazard had compared notes. So it was that Professor Alice Tay invited the Hazards to her campus. She arranged for them to have an apartment in the Women's College, surrounded by the green playing fields and gothic buildings built to resemble an English campus. Hazard's courses were to be his usual general introduction to Soviet law and a course for graduate law students and members of the Bar that compared the attitude towards civil rights in the socialist and American systems.

The Hazards left for Australia in February, 1978. They planned to stop off in Tahiti and New Guinea along the way. Both places were said to be paradises. Indeed Tahiti was, particulary Moorea. They spent a week along the grass covered-walls of an extinct volcano, which made for remarkable effects in combination with the water of the lagoons. New Guinea had been praised by friends as a museum of primitive peoples. Indeed it was, although there were cities which the Australians had built which looked like others in the developing world. For those who like places "at the end of the road," as Hazard did, the mountain country of Papua New Guinea was a delight. There was something to be learned of law too, because the country had just decided to abandon the Western law the Australians had introduced into the villages. The legal system was reverting to the grass hut and the village sage, which had been the traditional source of order.

While in Australia, the Hazards visited cities all over the Continent: Melbourne, Canberra, Adelaide, and even far away Perth. In each of them, Hazard lectured to the law faculty or political science department. Graduates of Columbia University were teaching at their universities. Australia was a common law country adhering closely to English tradition. Hazard enjoyed sitting below the statue of Queen Victoria in front of the law school overlooking the park in Sydney, and watching the barristers walk by dressed in traditional English wig and gown.

The students were not very different from those in the United States, except for their accents, which were hard to understand, and their lowered voices, which were hard to hear. Hazard learned that children were taught to keep their voices down, and Americans were identified in part by their strident tones. When Hazard collected his American dollars at the end of his term, in exchange for his Australian bank account, the clerk said he did not need to see a passport; he knew from the voice that it was a Yank who was talking.

On one occasion, Hazard was invited to testify before a committee of the parliament, which was investigating the state of human rights in the U.S.S.R. He was greeted at the Capitol by a most cordial group of Senators, one from each Australian state. They were almost caricatures of their home communities: the impeccably dressed Bond Street type man from Victoria; the business-type man from New South Wales, the self-assertive type from Queensland, and the cowboy diamond-in-the-rough from Western Australia. They heard him out in formal fashion, and then tendered him a memorable dinner in the Senatorial dining room.

There was time to walk endlessly through the streets of Sydney; to take the ferryboats across the bay to the beaches; to attend the concerts and plays in the Opera House with its sail-like roof, and to speak to small groups directed by professors, always in need of a visiting speaker. Sydney was fun; not exotic. It was like a blend of New York and London. Visitors could enjoy their stay, but it was not a vivid and shocking experience. One had the sense of being very far away from the world's events. The couple hung on to the morning BBC radio broadcasts in an effort to keep abreast of what was happening in their own world.

Louvain provided more of a contrast during the spring of 1979. On this occasion, Hazard was appointed a Fulbright professor, and was directed to teach in French. This made the term a difficult one, because three courses of formal magisterial lectures in a language other than his own required extensive preparation, and a considerable amount of attention. His students varied in age. He taught an entry level course which compared American and Soviet attitudes towards human rights. He gave a course for advanced students on the intervention of the state in what had traditionally been called matters of private law. This was also a comparison of U.S. and Soviet law. And, finally, a course for graduate students on problems met with in devising a socialist model for development.

Once again the Hazards were provided with an apartment on campus, but it was far different from the campus in Sydney. There were no great lawns, and no playing fields. It was a little city, constructed on what had been several farms a few years earlier, when the Belgian government had acceded to the demand of the citizens of the ancient city of Leuven to move the francophonic half of the University across the linguistic frontier in Belgium so that its students would not be speaking French in the streets of Leuven. To an American it was a silly fight between the two groups of Belgians, although one could understand the economic and social reasons for the split.

The new town on the rolling hills of Eastern Belgium, not far from Luxembourg, had been built in two styles: The laboratories and classrooms of the science faculties were at the top of the hill and built of white stone while the humanities were at the bottom in buildings constructed to look like the streets of a medieval town. The Hazards were in the medieval part, not more than five minutes from the Faculty of Law with its splendid new library and classroom building.

Students in Belgium were less communicative in class than those in Sydney. Their experience had been solely with magisterial lectures, and it was rare that a brave one would raise a hand to ask a question. One could not call upon anyone from the teacher's pulpit. It just was not done. This made for a passive relationship, but the youngsters were friendly, and they invited the Hazards to eat with them in the communal dormitories or in restaurants. Some even came to office hours, although the Belgian professors had warned Hazard that it was exceptional for a student to call upon a professor in his office. Hazard tried hard to persuade them to do so, and some did, especially if they wanted to discuss the possibilities of obtaining a scholarship for study in the United States.

The town offered little in the way of formal entertainment. The Faculty of Drama presented a monthly play in their theater, and these were well done, although hard to understand. There were some lectures on various themes and dinner invitations from professors but evenings were usually spent at home. There were occasional trips to Brussels to lecture or to see the museums; trips to Ghent to visit friends and to Leuven to lecture; and finally a memorable weekend with Viscount Walter Ganshoff Vandermeersch, the retired Prosecutor General of Belgium. He was a friend of many years because of his concern for comparative law, and his participation with Hazard in the International Faculty of Comparative Law.

Ganshoff had been the chief of Belgian intelligence in England during the war. He had stories to tell of those exciting days. He had been an intimate of the King of Belgium; had been decorated with the Order of the Bath; had sat as Judge on the European Court of Human Rights; and finally had been ennobled at the end of his brilliant career. He had built himself a small castle on the Belgo-Luxembourg frontier overlooking the pine forest where the "Battle of the Bulge" had occurred, Germany's last effort to halt the advancing Allied armies. The castle was impeccably maintained by his lady, who had been one of the Solvay family, with which Hazard's family had been associated long before in establishing the Solvay Process Company in Syracuse. It was one of those legendary weekends which cannot be duplicated in the United States.

Ganshoff took of his precious time to come on another weekend to Louvain to attend the ceremony which honored Hazard with the degree of doctor honoris causa. He joined other Belgian friends from the universities and the bench whom Hazard had come to know over the years. These dignitaries sat in front of the students on the high bench before the platform. The gowned professors made their way into the auditorium behind the rector, Msgr. Edouard Massaux. The latter was a noted Roman Catholic prelate. He regaled the group later, at a formal luncheon, with comments on his recent visit with the Pope to discuss a new decree on the Catholic universities, of which Louvain was one of the most prominent.

Hazard had to speak for his honors, and he gave an address on a comparison of Soviet and American attitudes toward comparative law. French was not his native language, and he took the precaution of writing out his thoughts and having them put in order by the young Assistant Registrar of the Law School. The audience seemed to understand, for, as Alphonse De Vries said later, the accent was understandable. De Vries was a Supreme Court judge who had formerly taught at the International College at Bruges and he was fluent in English, French, and Flemish. He knew how hard Hazard had worked.

The blue *épitoge* of Louvain, with its white fur border, was draped over Hazard's black gown, and the diploma was presented. The event was over, except for the luncheon. Hazard had been through the same procedure before at Lehigh, Freiburg, Leiden, and Paris; but only at Freiburg had he been required to make an address, and that was given in English, for he knew no German. Lehigh had provided a typical American university setting: a huge auditorium filled with graduating students, a prominent American, in this case William F. Buckley, to make the address, a rather long list of recipients of degrees, with the honoraries at the end, a pleasant luncheon with the President, Provost, and recipients with families, and departure.

Freiburg had been equally simple, indeed more so, for the degree had been awarded through the mails with the proviso that a speech would be necessary when Hazard could come to Freiburg. It proved to be convenient soon thereafter, and the Hazards went to one of their favorite German Universities. Hazard had once taught a summer school course there, in Soviet law, and had made many friends. Following the speech, there was a splendid luncheon in a prominent restaurant near the Cathedral, and it was over.

Leiden had been far more ceremonial, for the occasion was the 400th anniversary of the University. Hazard and his wife were flown over at University expense to take part in the elaborate proceedings. They began with a sprightly evening in the old University Hall, where a buffet was served while three different orchestras played in three adjacent rooms. The Hazards chose the gypsy orchestra made up of Dutch professors who liked Eastern European music as much as Hazard did and played it to perfection. Then there was the great ceremony in the Peterkirke where the Pilgrims had wintered before leaving for Plymouth. It was an enormous, historic, Gothic pile. The recipients were marched through the ancient streets of the city. Students hung out of the windows of old Dutch houses and crowded the sidewalks to take pictures. Finally, the Church was reached, the West doors thrown open, and the procession filed in.

In the front row before the pulpit sat the Queen of the Netherlands with her consort, Prince Bernhard and her daughter, Princess Beatrix, soon to become Queen on the abdication of her Mother. The entire family had studied at Leiden, and it was "their" University. Citations were spoken in the language of the recipient, in Hazard's case by Professor F.J.M. Feldbrugge, Director of the Documentation Center for East European Law. He was a noted specialist in Soviet law whom Hazard had come to know well through the years of exchanged visits. After the rector's address to the assemblage, the recipients filed out to a reception at the University dining hall. Every honoree was presented to the Queen and to her family. She was exactly Hazard's age, and quite the homebody that she had always been represented to be. The next day, the group was taken to Amsterdam to see the exhibition of the history of the University which had been arranged in the Museum. Afterwards, the Hazards left for home so that they could attend the 50th anniversary of the Yale Class of 1930; Hazard had to participate in the Class panel which he had arranged.

The ceremony in Paris was very moving. Hazard was reminded of his schoolboy days, when he had spent the summer living on the corner across from the Sorbonne, studying violin and French. It was like "coming home." This time, only Hazard attended, and he flew over for the occasion. It began with a ceremonial luncheon in the dean's apartment in the famous old Rue Soufflot Law Faculty building. The apartment was in Empire style, very suited to such an occasion. The white-gloved waiters stood behind every chair; the silver patterns of dishes that only a French chef could prepare were brought in. The President of Paris was a woman, for the first time, and she presided. Those who were to be honored were the Director General of UNESCO, a Senegalese, an English Don, a Spanish professor, a Pole, and Hazard.

In mid-afternoon, the group was taken to the great hall of the Sorbonne, and robed. It was immense. As the procession entered the hall, the string orchestra of the Garde Republicaine played French classical music. The lights were blinding on the stage because it was being televised. The rector of all of the newly created "universities" read an allocution; the UNESCO Director followed in response for the recipients; and then each one was called forward to receive the *épitoge* of Paris, designed by Napoleon to fit over the red gowns of the scholars. It was in red and blue with white fur trimming. The diploma was in a dark, red tube, accompanying the epitoge's box with golden clasps. Following the ceremony, the guests retired to the banquet hall upstairs, and Hazard's friends were there to greet him. Professor André Tunc, noted professor of comparative law, led the group. He was the professor chosen to write and read the amusing citation, which he said had been commanded by the President to last ten minutes. It was indeed long.

The academic year 1979-80 was spent on the Columbia campus with familiar routines but without committee meetings. Hazard attended the law faculty and the political science department's meetings, just to keep abreast of the fast changing concerns of professors. He remembered the comment that Philip C. Jessup made when he retired to become a Judge on the International Court of Justice at The Hague: he was not regretful of leaving, for the world of scholarship had passed him by with its new techniques and methods. He also commented on the new vocabulary of political science and the law.

Hazard had sensed the same transition from the days when he studied and began teaching to those of the 1970's. The scholarship was now turned toward computers and behavioral studies. Although Hazard had enjoyed his year in California at the Institute for Advanced Study of the Behavioral Sciences, he had not absorbed the technology. He still shuddered when he saw a computer print out. He preferred to have authors tell him the substance of their findings in simple prose to having to pour over columns of figures which told the story. He also found the new vocabulary hard to use, although it could be learned. Scholars were coining new words to indicate that they were evolving new concepts. They thought old words would be taken as symbols of old ideas, and they wanted to be on the frontier of knowledge. Sometimes, it seemed as if a scholar's reputation hinged on the new words he could coin. The readers of their books had to work through an introductory chapter of definitions to find the clue to the mystery that was to follow, cloaked as it was in an unfamiliar vocabulary.

A round-the-world teaching assignment came Hazard's way in the fall of 1980. It was not the first time the Hazards had sailed on the famous teaching ship which the Institute for Shipboard Education conducted for a series of sponsoring universities. This was their second voyage on the S.S. Universe, the first having been in the spring of 1974. The concept was a good one: the semester would be devoted to serious study of the regions of the world through which the ship sailed. University credit would be given for the courses, and the teachers were chosen to meet the standards of the sponsoring university. In the fall of 1980, the University of Colorado was the sponsor.

Hazard's job was to conduct three courses: international law, comparative politics, and political philosophy. He focused the first two on the developing world, through which the ship would be sailing for most of the voyage. Susan served as assistant librarian as she had in 1974. She took the morning shift, since the Hazards had no objection to rising early. In the evenings, there was a "community college," at which visiting scholars who boarded to ride only between one port and the next would speak; and there were educational programs taken from American television for showing on board. Most of these covered places that were visited by the ship and problems that were studied in class.

The ship remained at every port for four or five days. The students were given the opportunity to hear diplomatic briefings from the United States Embassy. They visited the local university to meet with the students and learn their concerns; they saw shrines, temples, and places of art to develop their understanding of different cultures. On the evening of sailing, they heard the music of the country performed by troups brought on board. It was a remarkably well planned program of education and fun. Some of the 500 students focused on the fun, but most were there to learn and not solely to surf at all of the beaches around the world.

For the Hazards, who had traveled to a great many countries, the trip was a chance to revisit familiar places. Perhaps the most exciting visit was a trip to Canton. Hazard revisited the University where he had been entertained by his Yale college mate, Don Stevenson, fifty years earlier. China had been heralded as having made great progress, but the Hazards were disappointed. Canton seemed as down at the heel as Odessa, in the U.S.S.R, had years ago. There were new token apartment houses, but they did not outweigh the familiar Chinese hovels. The Pearl River was a polluted cesspool. Only the great Park and Sun Yat-sen pavilion were kept in first class order. The city was obviously starved of resources.

The countryside looked better. It was a rich part of China, with adequate rain and good sun. The fields were well-tended, and the Collective Farm that they visited seemed to be a remarkable combination of traditional buildings and some new techniques. If the rest of the People's Republic looked like Canton, there could be hope for the future only in agriculture; and there was reason to wonder why the Soviet leadership was so worried about China's power. It seemed to be a society still far from the achievement of strength. Conversations with professors at the University suggested that the gap of the "Great Leap Forward" and the "Cultural Revolution," for which Mao's colleagues were being criticized at the time, could not be bridged quickly. China had a long way to go before it could compete with the West or the U.S.S.R.

By 1981, retirement activities as a Sovietologist had fallen into a routine. Some of the experiences of previous years were being relived. In 1981-82, the Hazards returned to Cambridge, where they had spent 1952-53. This time Hazard came to occupy Goodhart Lodge as the Goodhart Professor in Legal Science. He was to teach a course on Soviet law in the Faculty of Law, and prepare a volume of Goodhart Lectures on the role of Soviet jurists in managing change in the U.S.S.R. It ended with a trip in June with twenty students, to the U.S.S.R. and Poland, to introduce them to the fundamentals of the "family of socialist law." Soviet law had evidently become stabilized, but Polish law was in ferment. The restless population tried to force the Communist Party to accept proposals designed to introduce restraints on the arbitrary use of power. The Party had obviously emerged victorious, but the academics still seemed to believe that new institutions designed to restrain bureaucrats would emerge, even though the creation of a pluralistic society was not permitted.

In the fall of 1982, a third voyage around the world on the S.S. Universe, under the Semester at Sea, provided another chance to see what was happening to socialist ideas in the developing world. Among the visits was a trip to the University in Shanghai, People's Republic of China. The impressions of China formed two years earlier at Canton were reinforced: China was a poor country, but with Mao's death there was new hope among the academics that education would be restored to a place of honor and that this would help the Chinese to become a powerful people.

At the end of the voyage, the Hazards returned to New York to resume familiar routines at Columbia University, teaching Soviet law and public administration. It began to look as if Sovietology had become an established field; the more so since W. Averell Harriman, during the autumn of 1982 provided funds to Columbia to revitalize the Russian Institute as the W. Averell Harriman Institute of Advanced Studies of the Soviet Union. There were no longer doubts that Sovietology had become an established career, and the pioneers were being lionized for their courage in embarking upon the field a half a century earlier.

BIBLIOGRAPHY

BIBLIOGRAPHY

Soviet Housing Law (New Haven: Yale University Press, 1939), pp. iv, 178.

Editor and introduction, *Soviet Legal Philosophy*, transl. by Hugh W. Babb (Cambridge: Harvard University Press, 1951), pp. xxxvii, 465 (20th Century Legal Philosophy Series, Vol.V).

Cases and Readings in Soviet Law (New York: Parker School of Foreign and Comparative Law, Columbia University, 1950), p. 431 (with Morris L. Weisberg, with the collaboration of George C. Denney, Jr. and George Krynski).

Law and Social Change in the U.S.S.R. (London and Toronto: Stevens & Sons Limited and the Carswell Company Ltd., 1953), pp. xxiv, 310. Reprint ed. Westport, Connecticut: Hyperion Press, 1981.

> French transl.: *Le Droit et l'Evolution de la Société dans l'U.R.S.S.* (Paris: Librairie générale de Droit et de Jurisprudence, 1954), p. 409 (Vol.2 of *Le Droit Soviétique* by René David and John N. Hazard, Vol.8 in *Les Systèmes de Droit Contemporains*). Spanish transl. (text updated to December 31, 1962): Vol.2 of *El Derecho Sovietico* by René David and John N. Hazard (Buenos Aires: La Ley, 1964).

The Soviet System of Government (5th ed.; Chicago: University of Chicago Press, 1980), p. 330. (The Chicago Library of Comparative Politics) 1st ed. 1957, p. 256; 2d ed. 1960, p. 262; 3rd ed. 1964, p. 284; 4th ed. 1968, p. 273.

> Korean transl. (of 2d ed.) *The Soviet System of Government* (Seoul, Korea: Eul-Yoo Publishing Co. Ltd. 1963), p. 402.
> Swedish transl. (of 3d ed.): Hur Sovjet styres (Stockholm: Bokforlaget Aldus/Bonniers, 1965), p. 267.
> Indian edition (photo-offset of 4th ed.): *The Soviet System of Government* (New Delhi, India: Sterling Publishers (P) Ltd., 1971), p. 275.

Settling Disputes in Soviet Society: The Formative Years of Legal Institutions (New York: Columbia University Press, 1960), pp. xiv, 534. (Studies of the Russian Institute, Columbia University.) Reprint ed. New York: Farrar, Straus & Giroux (Octagon), 1978, (with new Preface), pp. ix, 534.

The Soviet Legal System: Fundamental Principles and Historical Commentary (3d ed.; Dobbs Ferry, New York: Oceana Publications, Inc., 1977), pp. xvii, 621, (with William E. Butler and Peter B. Maggs); 1st ed. under title: *The Soviet Legal System: Post-Stalin Documentation and Historical Commentary* (1962), pp. 595, (with

Isaac Shapiro). (Parker School Studies in Foreign and Comparative Law); 2d ed. under title: *The Soviet Legal System: Contemporary Documentation and Historical Commentary* (1969), pp. xvi, 560, (with Isaac Shapiro and Peter B. Maggs).

Communists and Their Law: A Search for the Common Core of the Legal Systems of the Marxian Socialist States (Chicago: The University of Chicago Press, 1969), pp. xvi, 560. (Studies of the Research Institute of Communist Affairs of Columbia University.)

Managing Change in the U.S.S.R.: The politico-legal role of the Soviet Jurist (The Goodhart Lectures, 1982) (Cambridge, London, New York, New Rochelle, Melbourne, Sydney: Cambridge University Press, 1983), pp. ix, 182.

CHRONOLOGY

CHRONOLOGY

1909 - Born, Syracuse, New York, January 5
1913-21 - Syracuse elementary schools
   (Montessori, Goodyear-Burlingame, Lincoln Public)
1921-26 - The Hill School, Pottstown, Pennsylvania
1926-30 - Yale College
1930-31 - Tour around the world
1931-34 - Harvard Law School
1934-39 - Fellow, Institute of Current World Affairs
   - at Moscow Juridical Institute, Feb. 1935 - Dec. 1937
   - at University of Chicago Law School, Jan. 1938 - March 1939
1941-46 - United States Government service
   (Lend-Lease Administration, Foreign Economic Administration, Department of State)
   Seconded to: - Vice-President Henry Wallace as special assistant on mission to U.S.S.R. and China, June - July, 1944
   - to United States Prosecutor in preparation of indictment of Axis criminals, London, July - Sept. 1945
1946-83 - Columbia University
   Professor of Public Law, 1946-76; Nash Professor of Law, 1976-77; Emeritus (in residence) 1977-
   Managing Editor, *The American Slavic and East European Review*, 1951-59

   - Appointments during sabbaticals and leaves:
      Fulbright Visiting Professor of Law, University of Cambridge and London School of Economics, fall 1952
      Visiting Professor, Institut des Hautes Etudes Internationales, Université de Genève, fall 1959
      Fellow, Institute for Advanced Study in the Behavioral Sciences, 1961-62
      Visiting Research Professor, University of Dakar, Dec. 1964 - Jan. 1965
      Visiting Professor of Law, University of Teheran, Nov. - Dec. 1966
      Senior Specialist, East-West Center, University of Hawaii, Jan. - June 1967
      Visiting Professor, Semester at Sea, Chapman College, Spring 1965

Visiting Professor of Law, University of Sydney, Feb. - May, 1978

Fulbright Visiting Professor of Law, Université Catholique de Louvain, Spring 1979

Visiting Professor, Semester at Sea, University of Colorado, fall, 1980

Arthur L. Goodhart Professor in Legal Science, University of Cambridge, 1981-82

Visiting Professor, Semester at Sea, University of Pittsburgh, fall, 1982

- Summer term teaching appointments:

University of Minnesota, 1947; Claremont Graduate School, 1948; Stanford University, 1951, 1953; University of Tokyo, 1956; University of Freiburg, 1966; Salzburg Seminar, 1971; University of San Diego-Université de Paris, 1980; University of San Diego-University of Warsaw, 1981.

- Lecturing appointments as a member of the International Faculty of Comparative Law (Strasbourg):

At Easter recess sessions in Strasbourg, 1962-82, and at summer recess sessions held at Universities of Helsinki, 1962; Mexico City, 1963; Trieste, 1963; Santiago de Compostelo, 1964, 1974; Liège, 1965; Concepción, Jan. 1966; Coimbra, 1965, 1966; Cagliari, 1967; Exeter, 1968; Pescara, 1968, 1972; Amsterdam, 1969, 1973; Torino, 1970; Lisbon, 1971; Salamanca, 1971; and Mondovi, 1975, 1976

INDEX

INDEX

A

Acheson, Dean G., 54, 59
Afchar, Hassan, 100
Alma Ata, 82
American Association for the Advancement of Slavic Studies, Inc., 94-95
American Slavic and East European Review, 94-95
Amfiteatrov, Gregorii N., 21, 24
Amtorg Trading Corp., 36, 58-59
Ancestors, xiv
Andrews, Charles, xi
Arab world, 4
Atheistic propaganda, 112-13

B

Baldwin, Todd & Young, 33
Bedbugs, 71-72
Belaev, Major General, 58
Bement, Howard, xv
Bergson, Abram, 90
Berle, Adolph A., 50
Bibliography, 129
Birth, ix
Blatchford, Ned, 5
Bliven, Bruce, 34
Books authored, 98-101
Bormann, Martin, 85-86
Borodin, Makhail, 26
Bowie, Robert R., 44
Bukharin, Nikolai I., 23, 26
Bullitt, William C., 26
Burma, 7-9
Burns, James H., 51, 56, 60-61

C

Cairo, 4-5
Cambodia, 9-10
Cathedral of the Savior, 111
Chance, as influence on career, ix, xvii
Chengtu, 75
Chiang Kai-shek, 65, 73-74
Chiang Kai-shek (Mme.), 73-74
Chicken Hill Mission, 106
Children, 45
China, 8, 10-11, 72-76, 124-25
Choi Balsang, 76
Chou En-lai, 74
Chronology, 133
Chungking, 73-75
Church liturgy, 107
Chuvakhin, Dmitri, 66
Civil War (U.S.), ix

Clay, Lucius D., 55
Comintern, 22
Comparative law, 83-86
Courting, 43-44
Current Digest of the Soviet Press, 93

D

Dallin, Alexander, 91-92
David, René, 98
Davies, Emlen, 26
Davies, Joseph P., 26
DeKalb, Emma, ix-x
DeKalb, Enoch, ix
DeMenthon, M., 83, 85
Dowding, Ella G., xii

E

East West Center, 101
Eddy, Sherwood, 107
Education, xii-xiv, 17-27
Edwards, W. Randle, 102
Emeritus activities, 117-25

F

Faymonville, Philip R., 49-51, 62
Feldbrugge, F.J.M., 122
Foreign Workers' Club, 22
Freiburg, 121
Freund library, *See* Heinrick Freund Library

G

Ganshoff Vandermeersch, Walter, 120-21
Gardner, John W., 91
George VI (king of England), 34
German-Japanese threat, 61
Goglidze, Sergei A., 66, 69, 72
Gromyko, Andrei A., 52
Groves, Leslie R., 55
Gruliow, Leo, 93

H

Hamson, Charles J., 98
Harper, Samuel N., 95
Harriman, W. Averell, 51, 65, 125
Hazard, Ada DeKalb, ix-xii
Hazard, Augusta Gerloff, xi
Hazard, John Gibson, ix-xi
Heinrick Freund Library, 99
Hill School, xii, 105-06
Hong Kong, 10
Honolulu, 12, 101

Hoopes, James P., 55-56
Hopkins, Harry, 49-53
House of Representatives Unamerican Activities Committee, 55, 56
Hudson, Manley O., xvi, 19
Hutchins, Robert M., 96

I

Institute for Advanced Study in the Behavioral Sciences, 100
Institute of Current World Affairs, xvi-xvii, 31
Irkutsk, 81
Islam, 112

J

Jackson, Robert, 81
Japan, 12
Jerusalem, 5
Jessup, Philip C., 123

K

Kiev, 4, 31
Kishinev, 32
Kohler, Foy, 91-92
Komsomolsk, 66-67
Koo, Wellington (Mme.), 11
Korea, 11
Korovin, Evgenii Aleksandrovich, 19, 24
Koussevitsky, Serge, 37
Kozhevnikov, F.I., 19
Krasnushkin, Evengii Konstantinovich, 18
Krasnushkina, Marta Abramovna, 18
Krasnoyarsk, 68
Krumm, John M., 108
Krylenko, Nikolai V., 23, 25
Krynsky, George, 97-98

L

Langer, William L., 89-91
Lattimore, Owen, 65, 73, 76
Law faculty: University of Dakar, 100; University of Paris, 122; University of Teheran, 100
Lawrence, Susan, 44-46
Lawrence, William A., 44
Leavell, Hugh R., 82
Leiden, 121-22
Lemkin, Raphael, 83
Lend-Lease, 49-62
Leningrad, 3, 17
Levi, Edward H., 96
Liberman, Bella Isaevna, 18
Lin Fu-shun, 101
Lipson, Leon, 56
Litvinov, Maxim, 57-58
Louvain, 119-21
Lukashev, Konstantin, 59

M

Magadan, 66
Manhattan Project, 55
Marriage, 41-46
Marshall, George C., 51
Martin, William MacChesney, 60, 89-90
Marxists' commitment, 22
McCarthy, Joseph R., 56
McGill, William J., 117
McKee, Elmore, 106
Meigs, Mrs. John, 105
Monnet, Jean, 54
Moore, Paul, Jr., 110
Moore, Thomas E., 3
Moscow, 3-4, 17-27
Moscow cathedral, See Cathedral of the Savior
Moscow Law Institute, 19-27
Mosely, Philip E., 90, 92
Musical education, xii, xv
Musser, John M., 3

N

Negotiating with the Soviets, 36
New Republic, 33-34
Nuremberg indictment, 81-86
Nurernberg tactics, 81

O

Oumansky, Constantin, 50

P

Pahlevi, Shah, 5-6
Palmer, Arthur E., 3
Pashukanis, Evgenii B., 21, 23-24
Passport problems, 56
Pearson, Lester, 54
Persia, 5
Philippines, 10
Pike, James, 108-09
Poland, 31-32, 34
Pratt, John, 53-54
Prison camps, 67

R

Radek, Karl B., 23, 26
Randolph, Philip, 107
Recognition of Soviet government, ix
Reese, Willis L.M., 67
Religion, 105-13
Rheinstein, Max, 95
Robinson, Geroid T., 89-92
Rockefeller Foundation, 90
Rogers, Walter S., xvii
Rose, Milton C., 33
Rudenko, See Soviet Government Purchasing Commission
Rudenko, Roman, 83

Rudzinski, Alexander W., 101
Russian Institute, 89-102
Russian Research Center of Harvard University, 91

S

S.S. Universe, 124
Sabbaticals, 99
St. George's Church, 108-11
Schley, Reeve, 57, 59
Scott, James Brown, xiv-xvi
Shawcross, Sir Hartley, 83-85
Shulman, Marshall D., 91
Siam, 9
Siberia, 65, 72
Simmons, Ernest J., 90, 94
Skvirsky, Boris, 52
Soskice, Frank, 83
Soviet Embassy, Chunking, 74
Soviet Government Purchasing Commission, 55, 58-59
Soviet law, similarity with West, 20
Soviet Protocol Committee, 54-55
Spalding, Sidney P., 53
Spykman, Nicholas J., xiv-xv
Stalgevich, A.K., 24
Stalin, Joseph V., 22, 26, 53
Stoessel, Walter J., Jr., 92
State trading, 59
Stettinius, Edward R., Jr., 53
Soong, T.V., 75
Sun Yat-sen (Mme.), 74
Sunday school, 105
Swasti (prince of Siam), 9
Sydney Law Faculty, 117-19

T

Tay, Alice E., 118

Taylor, Telford, 83-84
Tukhachevsky, Marshall M., 26
Tunc, André, 123

U

Unamerican Activities Committee, *See* House of Representatives Unamerican Activities Committee
UNESCO, 98
University of Chicago, 96-97
University of Dakar, *See* Law faculties
University of Paris, *See* Law faculties
University of Teheran, *See* Law faculties
Uranium, 55
Urumchi, 72-73

V

Vincent, John C., 65, 72, 74
Vyshinsky, Andrei Y., 23-24

W

Wall Street, 31-43
Wallace, Henry A., 65-77
Wallace, Schuyler, C., 90, 92
Wesson, Charles M., 55, 59-60
Willet, Joseph, 90
World War I's impact, ix

Y

Yale Hope Mission, 106
Yale University, xiv, 41
Young, Harold, 7-9

Z

Zweigert, Konrad, 99